MIGHTY MACHINES
Questions and Answers

This edition published by Parragon in 2008
Parragon
Queen Street House
4 Queen Street
Bath BA1 1HE, UK

ISBN 978-1-4075-5981-0

Printed in Indonesia

MIGHTY MACHINES
Questions and Answers

LIVE. LEARN. DISCOVER.

Written by Adam Hibbert, Chris Oxlade, and James Pickering
Expert consultant: Steve Parker

Bath · New York · Singapore · Hong Kong · Cologne · Delhi · Melbourne

Contents

CHAPTER ONE
RACING MACHINES

12 Who raced a horse and carriage in a train?

13 Who first raced in cars?

14 Who used a rocket to go faster than 600 mph?

14 Who put a rocket on a bike?

15 Who went faster than the speed of sound in a car?

16 Which cars race to a formula?

17 What's an Indy car?

17 Which cars race for 24 hours?

18 When is a saloon car not a saloon car?

18 What is stock car racing?

19 Who races through dirt and ice?

20 Who waves a checkered flag?

20 Who wears fireproof underwear?

21 Who works in the pit?

22 Which cars race in a straight line?

23 What is a funny car?

23 How fast can a drag bike go?

24 Who uses their knees to go around corners?

24 Which motorcycle racers have three wheels?

25 Which motorcycles don't have brakes?

26 Who races across the Sahara?

26 What are rally Karts?

27 Which racecourse has jumps?

28 Who raced hot rods along the street?

29 What were café racers?

29 Who wears a yellow shirt if he's winning?

30 Which race needs sunshine?

31 Which cars don't need gas?

31 How fast can a Sinclair C5 go?

32 Where do you come first if you are last?

33 Which race cars have no engines?

33 Are there races for trucks?

34 Who wears a crash helmet at sea?

34 Who's the fastest man on water?

35 Which boats use water jets?

36 Which record breaker had three hulls?

36 Who races on a cat?

37 Which boats skate on ice?

38 What were Gee Bees?

38 What was the longest air race?

39 When was the first air race?

CHAPTER TWO
SHIPS AND SUBMARINES

42 Who crossed the Atlantic on a bunch of reeds?

43 Who hollowed out logs?

43 Who went fishing in animal skins?

44 Who rowed for a long time in a longship?

45 Who rowed in battle?

45 Who steers an eight?

46 What were clippers?

47 What was a galleon?

47 Who went to sea on a junk?

48 Who sailed under the skull and crossbones?

48 What was a Corsairs' galley?

4

49 Who were Bonny and Read?

50 Which steamships had a tug-of-war?

50 What was the first steamboat?

51 Which steamers used paddles?

52 What was a steam liner?

52 Which modern liner has sails?

53 What does a tug do?

54 What is the biggest ship?

54 What is a ro-ro?

55 What is a container ship?

56 Which boat has wings?

57 Which boat flies?

57 Which ship has two hulls?

58 Who trawls the oceans?

58 What is a factory ship?

59 Who hunted whales?

60 Which boats are unsinkable?

61 What is a lightship?

61 Which boat puts out fires?

62 Which ship is a floating airfield?

63 What was a pocket battleship?

63 Which ship is invisible?

64 What is a yacht?

65 Which boats can travel the fastest?

65 Who surfs across waves?

66 How big are submarines?

66 What was a U-boat?

67 What is a periscope?

68 What is a micro sub?

69 What are Alvin and Jason Junior?

69 How deep can submersibles go?

CHAPTER THREE
CARS

72 What was a horseless carriage?

72 Who invented the first car?

73 Which was the first car to be sold?

74 Who got dressed up to go motoring?

75 What was a "Tin Lizzie?"

75 Who spoke to the driver through a tube?

76 Who drove a Silver Ghost?

76 Which car was very cheap to run?

77 Who went on trips in a charabanc?

78 Who were the Bentley Boys?

79 What did the movie stars of the 1930s drive?

79 Who used fast cars to get away?

80 What was the "Tin Goose?"

80 Why was the Citroën 7CV so special?

81 What was the people's car?

82 Which car could really fly?

83 Which car had gull wings?

83 What was a T-bird?

84 Who drove around in a bubble?

84 What is a smart car?

85 What is a Mini?

86 Who flames their cars?

87 What is a lowrider?

87 What is a street rod?

88 What is a sports car?

88 Which sports car is still handmade?

89 Which powerful car was named after a wild horse?

90 What was Willys jeep?

90 What is four-wheel drive?

91 Which car can swim?

92 How do robots make cars?

92 Who crash tests cars?

93 How are cars designed?

94 What is an internal combustion engine?

95 Why do cars have gears?

95 What are springs and shock absorbers?

96 Which car had an ejector seat?

97 Who had his Rolls–Royce painted in amazing flowery patterns?

97 Which supercar had six wheels?

98 Which car can shorten itself?

98 Which car makes water?

99 Which car runs on sunlight?

CHAPTER FOUR
TRAINS

102 Which train was pulled by horses?

102 Which train was the first to carry passengers?

103 What was the first train engine?

104 How do trains fit together?

104 What's a locomotive?

105 Who steers the train?

106 How is the steam made?

106 How does steam power work?

107 When was steam power used?

108 Which diesel was a "centipede?"

108 Why did diesel take over from steam?

109 Which diesel looked like an airplane?

110 Which country went electric first?

110 What's a pantograph?

111 Are electric engines better than diesel?

112 What is a chaldron?

112 Which train was the most luxurious?

113 What's a Pullman?

114 Who rode on a wooden track?

114 How are tracks laid?

115 Which train was pushed by air?

116 Which trains travel by cables?

116 Where is the longest straight?

117 Can trains travel the length of Africa?

118 Is the Channel Tunnel longest?

118 How do trains cross rivers?

119 Where was the first raised city railroad?

120 Who slept in the "Tube?"

120 When were trains first used in war?

121 What train is a tank?

122 What was the biggest train crime?

122 Do trains crash?

123 Did railroad projects always work?

124 Can any trains travel upside down?

125 Which train can climb a volcano?

125 Do toy trains ever crash?

126 How long is the longest train?

126 Which train is fastest?

127 Which train travels farthest?

128 Which train flies?

128 What is a bullet train?

129 Are trains "green?"

CHAPTER FIVE
MOTORCYCLES

132 Who was the first to put pedals on a bike?

132 What was a penny farthing?

133 What was a safety bicycle?

134 Which bike had a steam engine?

134 Who put an engine above a front wheel?

135 What did the first motorcycle look like?

136 What is a driveshaft?

136 What were leather belts for?

137 When was a drive chain first used?

138 Who were Harley and Davidson?

138 Why was Brough superior?

139 What was an Indian?

140 Where is a motorcycle's engine located?

140 Are motorcycle engines all the same shape?

141 What is a two-stroke engine?

142 What is a hog?

142 What is a sidecar?

143 What is a Gold Wing?

144 What is a scooter?

144 Which is the best-selling motorcycle ever?

145 Which scooter fits in a car trunk?

146 What is a trials bike?

146 Which motorcyclists wear armor?

147 Which bikes have knobbly tires?

148 Who had a holster on a Harley?

149 Who dropped from the sky with mini bikes?

149 Who had machine guns on their motorcycles?

150 What is a TT race?

150 Who raced on wooden boards?

151 What is a superbike?

152 What is a chopper?

153 Who reached 214 mph on a Triumph?

153 Who put three engines on a motorcycle?

154 How do you go faster on a motorcycle?

154 How do you slow down?

155 How do you change gear?

155 Why do motorcyclists lean over on corners?

156 Which racing bike has no front forks?

157 Which bike do you sit in?

157 Which bike crossed the USA using less than 15 gallons of fuel?

158 What is stunt riding?

158 What is the wall of death?

159 What is freestyle motocross?

CHAPTER SIX
TRUCKS AND DIGGERS

162 Which trucks had steam engines?

162 What did trucks look like before steam engines were invented?

163 What was a charabanc?

164 What is a cab-over truck?

165 What is the fifth wheel?

165 What gives piggyback rides?

166 How do truck drivers talk to each other?

167 Where do truckers sleep?

167 What is a jackknife?

168 What is a monster truck?

169 Who paints trucks for protection?

169 What are customized trucks?

170 What is a dragster truck?

170 What is the fastest truck?

171 Can trucks do wheelies?

172 How do tanks travel?

172 Which trucks can swim?

173 What carries missiles?

174 Which truck scrapes?

174 What is a digger?

175 Which are the biggest trucks in the world?

176 Which digger can do different jobs?

177 Which trucks can reach high up?

177 How is concrete delivered?

178 What are chains used for?

179 Which trucks race across the Sahara?

179 What is four-wheel drive?

180 Can trucks move houses?

180 Which truck carried a spacecraft?

181 Which trucks have dozens of wheels?

182 Which fire truck has two drivers?

183 How far can a fire truck's ladder reach?

183 Who puts aircraft fires out?

184 What is a wrecker?

185 Which truck saves lives?

186 How do loggers load logs?

186 What is a road train?

187 What is a straddle truck?

188 What needs a ramp to unload?

189 Which truck tows aircraft?

189 Which trucks carry trash?

CHAPTER SEVEN
AIRCRAFT

192 Who were the first people to fly?

192 Who built a steam plane?

193 Who flew the first gliders?

194 Who made the first airplane flight?

195 What is a monoplane?

195 Who was the first to fly across the English Channel?

196 Which airship burst into flames?

196 Who flew the first airship?

197 Are airships used today?

198 Who was the Red Baron?

199 What were barnstormers?

199 Who were the first people to fly across the Atlantic?

200 Who made the first solo flight across the Atlantic?

201 Who was the first to fly across the Pacific?

201 Which woman flew solo from England to Australia?

202 Which plane is also a boat?

203 How fast could seaplanes go?

203 How do planes land on snow?

204 Which planes have a hook?

204 What was a flying fortress?

205 Who attacked out of the Sun?

206 Who invented the jet engine?

207 What was the first jet plane?

207 What was the first jet airliner?

208 Which fighter can swing its wings?

209 Which plane is invisible?

209 Which plane has back-to-front wings?

210 Which airliners carry the most people?

210 Which is the biggest plane?

211 Which transatlantic airliners have only two engines?

212 Which plane traveled at 4,500 mph?

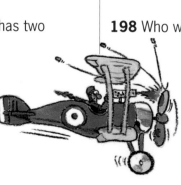

212 Which plane had no wings?

213 Which is the fastest jet?

214 Which jet plane can hover?

214 Which planes can take off and land in cities?

215 Which plane can swivel its engines?

216 Why are helicopters used for rescuing people?

216 Who invented the first true helicopter?

217 What is an autogyro?

218 Which airplanes have no engines?

218 Who hangs from a glider?

219 Who flies on hot air?

CHAPTER EIGHT
SPACECRAFT

222 Who made the first liquid fuel rocket?

223 What did the first satellite do?

223 Who was the first earthling in space?

224 What was the biggest rocket ever?

224 What do rockets carry?

225 Why do rockets have stages?

226 Who was the first person in space?

226 Who was the first American in space?

227 Who made the first space walk?

228 Who was the first person on the Moon?

229 Who took a car to the Moon?

229 For whom was the number 13 unlucky?

230 How do you fit into a space suit?

231 Who trains in a water tank?

231 Why do astronauts need space suits?

232 Who returned to Earth at 38,600 mph?

232 Who parachuted into the ocean?

233 Which space travelers had ejector seats?

234 What do astronauts eat?

235 How long can you stay in space?

235 How do you go to the bathroom in space?

236 Which spacecraft is reusable?

236 What is an MMU?

237 What does the space shuttle do?

238 What is a satellite?

238 How do satellites stay up?

239 Do satellites ever fall out of the sky?

240 Is there a telescope in space?

241 What happens if the telescope breaks down?

242 Which voyagers visited all the planets?

242 Which probe got too hot?

243 Which probe visited a comet?

244 What bounced around on Mars?

244 Who drove a vehicle on Mars?

245 Did Vikings really land on Mars?

246 Who is building a new space station?

247 Will there ever be a Moon base?

247 Will you ever go to space?

248 What will spacecraft be like in the future?

249 Will we ever visit other solar systems?

249 Will we colonize Mars?

250 Glossary

253 Index

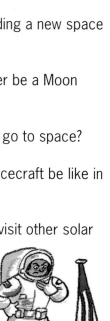

CHAPTER ONE

RACING MACHINES

? Who raced a horse and carriage in a train?

In 1825, George Stephenson raced his engine Locomotion against a team of horses, and won. For the first time ever, he showed that a mechanical vehicle could travel more quickly than a horse-drawn carriage.

Locomotion

Amazing! Racing machines have been around for a very long time. The Romans used to race horse-drawn chariots more than 2,000 years ago. Their chariots had two wheels that were connected by a wooden axle. It must have been a bumpy ride. The drivers used to stand up to drive, for balance. The more horses, the faster the chariot went.

Is it true?
In 1897, a cyclist beat a motorcyclist in a race.

YES. A man called W. J. Stocks pedaled over 27 miles on his bicycle in one hour, and beat a motorcycle by 300 yards. The rider of the motorcycle was not happy. He said that the crowd was too noisy and had distracted him!

Early motor race, France 1902

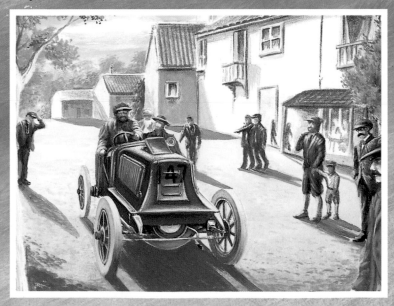

Who first raced in cars?

The first ever race was in 1894 between Paris and Rouen in France. The Count de Dion won in a steam-powered car, which could only manage 11 mph. Early motor races showed people that cars were as fast and reliable as horses.

? Who used a rocket to go faster than 600 mph?

In 1970, American Gary Gabelich drove his rocket-powered car, The Blue Flame, at 630 mph through the Bonneville Salt Flats, and it's still the world's fastest rocket car. When he wasn't breaking records, Gary also raced dragsters and worked as a test astronaut.

Thrust SSC

? Who put a rocket on a bike?

Richard "Rocketman" Brown started building The Challenger in 1996. It had three rocket engines, which produce about 12,200 horsepower per ton, taking it to 200 mph!

Challenger

Rocket-powered car

Is it true?
Some cars need parachutes.

YES. Some cars are so fast that brakes alone aren't powerful enough to stop them. Parachutes drag these cars back to lower speeds when they're traveling very quickly. Thrust SSC has four parachutes to bring it back below the sound barrier.

? **Who went faster than the speed of sound in a car?**
Briton Andy Green set a world record in 1997, when he drove the jet-powered Thrust SSC at 763 mph through the Nevada desert.

Gobron-Brillié

Amazing! As early as 1904, some cars could travel at more than 100 mph! Louis Rigolly was the first person to reach this speed in his enormous 100 horsepower Gobron-Brillié car, during the July Speed Trials in Ostend, Belgium. Luckily he didn't crash. Seat belts hadn't been invented, and Rigolly only wore a cloth cap to protect his head!

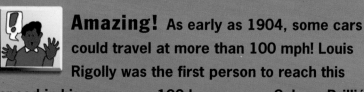

Amazing! Although go-karts are much smaller than other racing cars, they can reach speeds of up to 150 mph! Karting is very popular among young drivers, and many Formula One stars, such as Michael Schumacher and Lewis Hamilton, used to race karts.

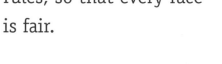

Which cars race to a formula?

There are very strict formulas or rules about how race cars are built. Formula One cars' size, shape, and gas tank are all governed by rules, so that every race is fair.

Ferrari Formula One race cars

Is it true?
Modern race cars have wings.

YES. They are at the front and back of the car. A race car's wings are carefully designed to stop the car from taking off. As air passes over the wing, it pulls the car down onto the track. This gives the driver better control.

Indy car

? What's an Indy car?

Indy car racing takes place at the Indianapolis Motor Speedway. Indy cars have powerful engines and huge fins.

Le Mans sports car

? Which cars race for 24 hours?

Sports cars race around the Le Mans circuit in France for 24 hours. Two or three drivers take turns at the wheel to drive the car as far as possible.

? When is a saloon car not a saloon car?

When it's competing in the saloon car championships. The cars in these races look like the family cars you might see on the street, but underneath their bodywork is a specially built, very fast racer.

Saloon cars

 Amazing! Modern saloon racers lift themselves into the air on tall stilts! Like all race cars, saloon cars have to make regular pit stops during races. Repairs, adjustments, and tire changes need to be made as quickly as possible. These stilts save the mechanics from having to crawl under the car.

? What is stock car racing?

In the United States, stock car racing is organized by the National Association for Stock Car Auto Racing. Stock cars look like ordinary road cars, but they have much more powerful engines and extra safety features.

Stock cars

Is it true?
All stock cars have doors.

NO. The body shell of a stock car is in one piece. This reduces the weight of the car and improves safety. There's no glass on the driver's side either, so he or she has to climb in and out of the car through the empty window!

? Who races through dirt and ice?

Rally cars are built to compete in races on muddy tracks, across country, and even through snow. In such slippery conditions, accidents can happen, and often do!

Rally car

? Who waves a checkered flag?

Race officials aren't allowed to talk with drivers during a race, so they communicate with flags. Different flags warn of danger, problems, or may order a driver off the track. The checkered flag is waved in front of the winning car.

| End of race | Danger | Mechanical problems | All clear | The race has been stopped |

? Who wears fireproof underwear?

Underneath their overalls, racing drivers wear fire-resistant "Nomex" underwear, made up of a long-sleeved top, full-length pants, socks, and a balaclava. These protect the driver against a blaze of 1,480°F for over 10 seconds.

Amazing! In dry conditions, bald tires provide better grip than tires with grooves. In the rain, cars switch to tires with deep slots to disperse as much water as possible and prevent skids. Each tire can disperse 6 gallons of water from the road per second!

Unlike today's F1 cars, early models had no wings.

 Is it true?
Race cars could race across the ceiling.

YES. The air pressure pushing a speeding race car on to the track is so great that they could race upside down.

Unsportsman-like behavior

Slippery track

Designated car must stop at pits

A driver wants to overtake

Slow vehicle on track

Pit crew

? **Who works in the pit?**
About 20 mechanics work in the pits, where they make quick repairs and adjustments during a race. They can change a wheel in under five seconds!

Dragster

Amazing!
Dangerous things can happen at 300 mph. A blowover is when the front wheels lift off the ground and the whole car flips over backward! Modern dragsters have a safety device called a wheelie bar to keep the car on solid ground.

? Which cars race in a straight line?

Dragsters are specially built racers, which look and perform like nothing you would ever see on the road. A drag race is a noisy hurtle down a straight quarter-mile track, at more than 330 mph! Dragsters are designed with only one thing in mind—acceleration.

Pro Stock drag bike

What is a funny car?

Funny cars are bizarre looking versions of family cars that take part in some drag races. The bodywork is stretched out of shape, to fit over a huge supercharged engine and chassis. They're decorated with bright colors and patterns.

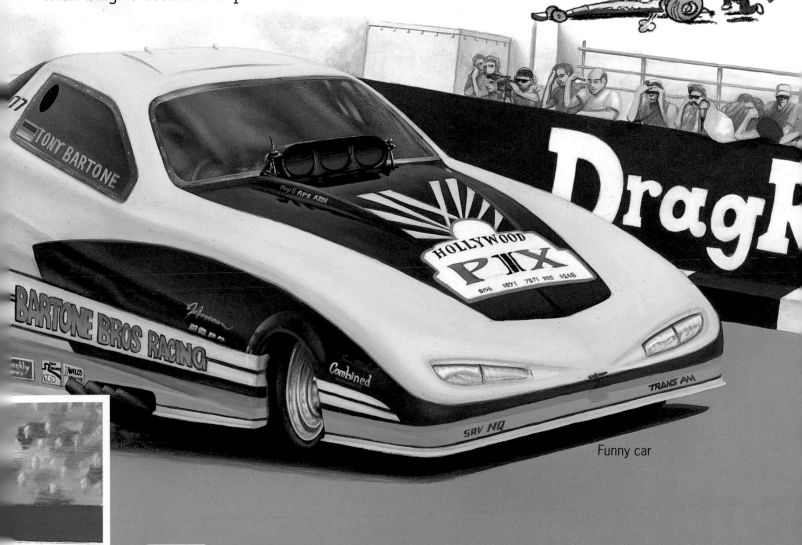

Funny car

How fast can a drag bike go?

Pro Stock drag bikes are two wheeled dragsters, or four wheelers, if you count their two rear stabilizers, which help to control them at high speeds. Drag bike ace Larry McBride has reached speeds of over 240 mph.

Who uses their knees to go around corners?

Riders in motorcycle Grands Prix take corners very quickly by leaning sharply into bends, scraping their knee against the track. This is called the "knee down" position. For protection, they have tough nylon knee pads sewn into their leathers.

Sidecar racing bikes

 ## Which motorcycle racers have three wheels?

Sidecar race bikes have three wheels. The sidecar isn't powered, but the second rider provides vital balance. On corners, the sidecar rider leans out for extra control, and the driver hardly has to reduce speed.

Amazing! Some bikes have tires with metal spikes sticking from them for riding on ice. The spikes pierce the icy surface and stop the bike from skidding. Without them, both bike and rider would go flying!

Knee down position

 Is it true?
Motorcycle races last only one hour.

NO. Different races have different lengths. The famous Le Mans race in France, for example, lasts for an exhausting 24 hours, while speedway races are often run over just four laps (1,300 yards) and last for about a minute!

 Which motorcycles don't have brakes?

Speedway race bikes don't have brakes. Instead, the bike slows to an almost instant halt as soon as the throttle is released. Riders wear extra sturdy steel boots, which they grind into the dirt, to bring the bike to a final standstill.

Speedway racing bikes

? Who races across the Sahara?

Competitors in the Dakar Rally set off from the French capital of Paris and race for 20 days, until they reach the capital of Senegal, West Africa. Cars have to withstand extremes of temperature, and the rigors of traveling through the dust and sand of the Sahara.

Amazing! In trials competitions, high speeds are not allowed! Trials riders jump over obstacles, with penalties for putting a foot on the ground. They mustn't go faster than 15 mph.

Rally karts

? What are rally karts?

Rally karts are speedy four wheeled, outdoor go-karts, designed for cross-country racing. They have wide tires to cope with bumpy ground, powerful engines, and roll cages, in case of an accident!

Paris-Dakar Rally

Is it true?
Some bikes have three wheels.

YES. Many ATVs (All Terrain Vehicles) have three wheels. They can be raced or used on farms for getting around safely and quickly. Quad bikes have four wheels, with thick tires and improved suspension.

? Which racecourse has jumps?

There are plenty of jumps and bumps on cross-country motorbike scrambles or motocross. Riders roar across the toughest terrain there is, through muddy woods, fields, and even snow!

Motocross

? Who raced hot rods along the street?

There used to be a dangerous trend in the United States for racing at night through the streets in souped-up road cars, nicknamed "hot rods." The official sport of hot rod racing was founded to put an end to racing on the highway.

Hot rods

Monte Carlo Grand Prix

✓✗ Is it true?
Race cars are not allowed to race in cities anymore.

NO. Several Grands Prix are still run on public streets. The event at Monte Carlo has been held on almost exactly the same circuit since 1929. The Australian Grand Prix in Melbourne is another example. The streets are cleared of public traffic in advance and crash barriers are set up. Dozens of classic car rallies also run from town to town.

What were café racers?

Café racers were specially modified bikes, which were raced to and from roadside cafés. This craze started in England in the 1960s. Not surprisingly, café racing on public highways is against the law!

Who wears a yellow shirt if he's winning?

The overall leader in the exhausting Tour de France bicycle race wears a bright yellow shirt. Recently, some stages of the race have been run in southern England, Spain, and Belgium, as well as France.

Amazing! In July 1924, Ernest Eldridge broke the World Land Speed Record on a French public street. He was driving a specially built 1908 Fiat called Mephistopheles and reached 146 mph!

Mephistopheles

29

❓ Which race needs sunshine?

There's a race every year in Australia for sunshine, or solar-powered, cars. The Sunraycer is one contender, with dozens of solar cells across its bodywork. These recharge its batteries and power the electric motor. The Sunraycer crossed the country at an average speed of 24 mph.

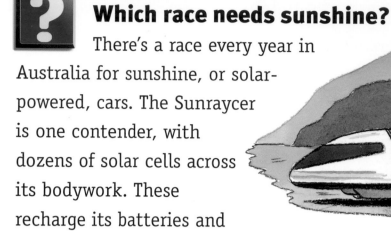

Violent Violet

☑☒ Is it true?

Violent Violet broke the electric speed record.

YES. In the 1990s superbike Violent Violet managed a speed of 99 mph to become the world's fastest electrically powered motorcycle. Better electric motors and lighter batteries mean that modern electric bikes can exceed 150 mph.

The Belgian Bullet

Amazing! In 1899, one electric car could easily outperform any gasoline-driven vehicle. Belgian Camile Jenatchy invented a magnetic motor and put it in a torpedo-shaped car, nicknamed The Belgian Bullet. The car took him to a speedy 65 mph!

? Which cars don't need gasoline?

Electric and solar-powered cars don't use gasoline. Since the 19th century, people have built cars that don't burn liquid fuel. Unfortunately, they can be less reliable and slower than gasoline-driven vehicles.

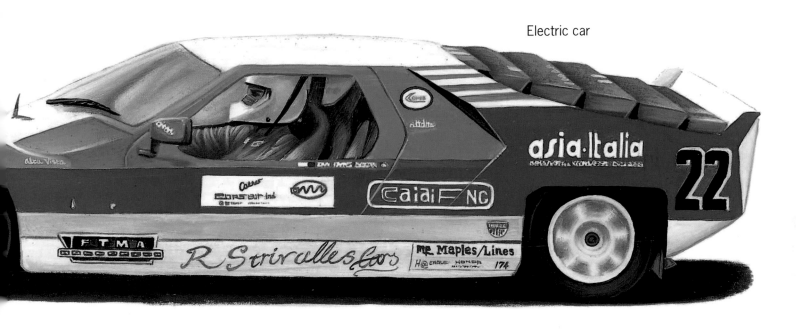

Electric car

? How fast can a Sinclair C5 go?

In 1996, Adam Harper attempted to reach 150 mph, and break the British electric car land speed record, in Alien, a modified, electric Sinclair C5.

Alien

Where do you come first if you are last?

A demolition derby is not so much a race as a test of strength. Modified road cars deliberately smash into one another, and the winner is the last car to keep moving. It's a dangerous sport, and drivers are protected by harnesses and safety cages.

Amazing!
Some tractors are powered by aircraft engines! Tractor tuggers have to drag a sled weighing a hefty 100 tons, for 100 yards along a dirt track.

Tractor tugger

Gravity Formula One

Gravity Formula One cars are downhill racers that have no engines, just a steering lever and a small brake. Drivers skid them down steep mountain roads at speeds of around 60 mph!

Demolition derby

Is it true?
People race lawn mowers.

YES. Some people really do take their lawn mowers racing. It's cheaper than Formula One, and it keeps the grass down as well. It just goes to show that if it's got wheels, someone out there will race it!

Racing trucks

Are there races for trucks?
Yes. Specially tuned trucks compete on racetracks. They look like ordinary trucks on the road, but they're a lot faster. Some even have jet engines, reaching speeds of over 350 mph!

Who wears a crash helmet at sea?

Powerboat drivers have to wear crash helmets. Powerboats are made from tough aluminum and each crew member is attached to a cord, which cuts the engine if they fall out. These boats can reach 150 mph (130 knots)!

Amazing! Powerboats can take off. At high speed, air can become trapped beneath them, lifting the boat above the water, with disastrous results.

Powerboat

Who's the fastest man on water?

Kenneth Warby managed an official speed of 306 mph (276 knots) in his hydroplane Spirit of Australia in 1978, on Blowering Dam in Australia.

Hydroplane

? Which boats use water jets?

Jet boats and Jet Skis use water jets to power them. In the same way that the jet engine of an aircraft forces hot gas backward, sending the plane forward, a water jet pushes pressurized water backward, driving the boat forward. Bumpy but a lot of fun!

Jet Ski

Is it true?
Some boats are powered by fans.

YES. Used in swamps and shallow water, airboats are powered by a fanlike propeller, mounted in a protective cage above the boat. Underwater propellers would get clogged with weeds in a swamp.

Which record breaker had three hulls?

In 1993, the three-hulled Yellow Pages Endeavour broke the sail-powered water speed record. With an airfoil sail perched on its tiny hulls, Yellow Pages Endeavour had a speed of 46.53 knots and a crew of just two, who traveled in a closed cockpit. Today's sailboats can reach speeds of 49 knots.

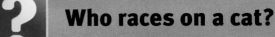

36

Who races on a cat?

Catamarans, or "cats" for short, are twin-hulled boats that can be raced, sailed for pleasure, or used as passenger boats. They travel through the water more easily than single-hulled boats, and are steadier in rough seas.

Sand yachts

 Amazing! Some boats race all the way around the world, using only wind power. The Round The World Yacht Race is held every four years. Highly skilled sailors can even race "the wrong way" around the world, against the wind and currents.

 ## Is it true?
People race yachts on land.

YES. Three-wheeled sand yachts race along beaches at about 75 mph. Other yachts race along disused railroad tracks, and even across snow!

? Which boats skate on ice?
Iceboats can reach speeds of more than 130 mph. They look like normal racing yachts, with tall sails and long ropes. But instead of hulls, they have skates that glide across the ice.

Iceboats

? What were Gee Bees?

American Gee Bee planes raced during the 1930s. The company that made them was called Granville Brothers (G. B.). These short, fat planes used to race at speeds of nearly 300 mph, in 5,500-mile-long races! Plane races were run to show how reliable the aircraft were.

MacRobertson race

? What was the longest air race?

The longest air race was the MacRobertson race from Mildenhall, England, to Melbourne, Australia, in 1934. It was won by the crew of a de Havilland in a time of 70 hours and 54 minutes.

Is it true?
The first nonstop flight around the world was made in 1933.

NO. Wiley Post did make the first solo around-the-world flight in Winnie Mae in 1933, but he had to stop several times to refuel. It was a 15,596-mile journey, and it took him just over a week.

Winnie Mae

Amazing! The first nonstop around-the-world flight wasn't until 1986. It took Dick Rutan and Jeana Yeager nine days to make the 24,000-mile journey. Their lightweight airplane Voyager had just 18 gallons of fuel left when it landed at Edwards Airforce Base.

Gee Bees

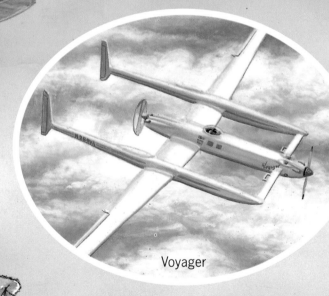

Voyager

When was the first air race?

The first air race was in 1909, near Reims in France. It took place only six years after the very first flight by the Wright brothers.

CHAPTER TWO

SHIPS & SUBMARINES

Who crossed the Atlantic on a bunch of reeds?

In 1970, Thor Heyerdahl, a Norwegian scientist and explorer, and his seven crew, crossed the Atlantic Ocean in a sailing boat made from reeds. The trip showed that sailors from ancient Egypt could have made the journey in reed boats thousands of years before Christopher Columbus in 1492.

Papyrus reed boat Ra II

 ## Is it true?
Dugout canoes are still used today.

YES. Dugouts are still made and used in many parts of the world. They are used for fishing and paddling along rivers. Fishermen who live on islands in the Pacific, such as Tonga, sail out to sea in dugout canoes with outriggers (small side hulls), which help the canoe to balance.

Who hollowed out logs?

Ancient people made boats called dugout canoes by hollowing out large tree trunks. They scraped and chipped the wood out with simple tools. Dugout canoes were amongst the first types of boat.

Dugout canoe

Amazing!
Boats called quaffas, which were sailed on the Euphrates River in Syria and Iraq, were made like baskets. In fact, the word *quaffa* means "basket." The boats were made of branches woven together and covered in tar. Large quaffas could carry 20 passengers.

Coracle

Who went fishing in animal skins?

Fishermen in Wales and Ireland used to go fishing in small boats called coracles or curraghs. They were made by covering a framework of bendy sticks with animal skins. A few fishermen still use canvas coracles today.

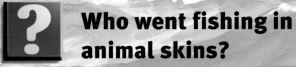

Viking longship

Who rowed for a long time in a longship?

About 1,000 years ago, Viking warriors rowed their longships when the wind blew from the wrong direction, or stopped blowing altogether. Longships were sleek wooden ships with a single square sail, used for exploring and launching raids.

Is it true?
Boats can be rowed with one oar.

YES. Some boats, such as gondolas in Venice, are rowed with a single oar. The rower stands at the boat's stern (back) and rows by sweeping a long oar from side to side.

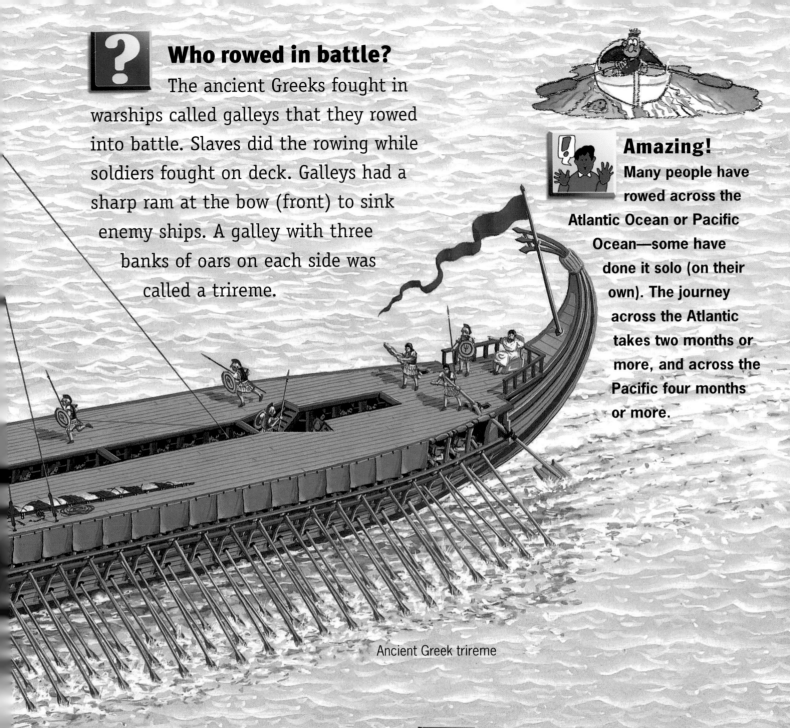

? Who rowed in battle?

The ancient Greeks fought in warships called galleys that they rowed into battle. Slaves did the rowing while soldiers fought on deck. Galleys had a sharp ram at the bow (front) to sink enemy ships. A galley with three banks of oars on each side was called a trireme.

Ancient Greek trireme

! Amazing!

Many people have rowed across the Atlantic Ocean or Pacific Ocean—some have done it solo (on their own). The journey across the Atlantic takes two months or more, and across the Pacific four months or more.

Rowing eights

? Who steers an eight?

An "eight" is the crew of a racing rowing boat. The ninth member, the cox, tells the rowers what pace to row at, and steers with a small rudder at the back of the boat.

45

What were clippers?

A clipper was a fast-sailing cargo ship. Clippers were built in North America and Europe in the 19th century to carry important cargoes, such as tea from China, quickly around the world. Clippers had three or four tall masts with five or more huge sails on each mast.

Clippers

Amazing! Large sailing ships often had a carving called a figurehead at the bow. Some figureheads were gods or saints, some were mythical sea creatures, such as mermaids, and some were real people. Viking longships had frightening dragon or snake figureheads.

Mayflower

❓ What was a galleon?

Galleons were trading and fighting ships used in the 15th and 16th centuries. The galleon Mayflower took the first pilgrims to North America in 1620.

❓ Who went to sea on a junk?

Chinese sailors have been going to sea in ships called junks for more than a thousand years. Junks have cloth sails strengthened with bamboo poles. Large junks have five masts. Junks were the first ships to have a rudder to help them steer.

Chinese junk

Who sailed under the skull and crossbones?

The skull and crossbones was the flag of pirates, who flew it from their ships. Pirates attacked ships especially in the Mediterranean and Caribbean. They often killed the crew, stole the cargo, and sometimes the ship itself!

 ### Amazing!
The famous pirate Blackbeard set off firecrackers in his huge beard to frighten people. Blackbeard's buried treasure has never been found.

What was a Corsairs' galley?

Corsairs were pirates in the Mediterranean about 400 years ago. They sailed in galleys, rowed by slaves chained to their oars.

Skull and crossbones

Is it true?
Sailors slept in beds.

NO. Ordinary sailors slept in hammocks, which hung from the deck above. Only the captain and officers had real beds in their cabins.

Bonny and Read

Who were Bonny and Read?

Mary Read and Anne Bonny were a famous pirate team. Read ran away to sea disguised as a boy and Bonny joined a pirate ship at the age of 16. They met when Bonny's ship captured Read's.

Which steamships had a tug-of-war?

In 1845, two British naval steamships had a tug of war, to see if propellers were better than paddles for making a ship move through the water. HMS Rattler, with a propeller, pulled HMS Alecto, which had paddles, backward at nearly three knots.

HMS Rattler

Is it true?

A ship's speed is measured in knots.

YES. One knot is equal to 1.15 mph. Sailors used to measure speed by dropping a log tied to a rope overboard and counting how quickly the knots tied in the rope went by.

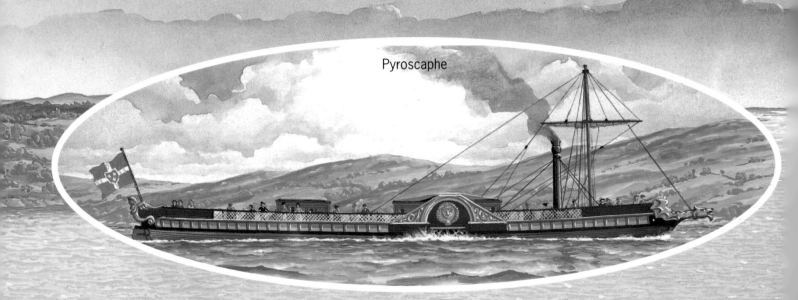
Pyroscaphe

What was the first steamboat?

The first boat to be propelled by a steam engine was called Pyroscaphe. It was built in France by Jouffroy d'Abbans, and had two paddle wheels. In 1783, it worked for just 15 minutes before it fell apart because of the thumping movement of the engines.

HMS Alecto

Amazing!

The steamship Great Eastern had three types of power—sails, paddle wheels, and a propeller. It was built by Isambard Kingdom Brunel and launched in 1858. At the time it was the largest ship in the world.

? Which steamers used paddles?

Before propellers were invented, most steamships used paddles driven by steam engines. Paddle steamers on the Mississippi River have one large stern paddle, which works very well in shallow water.

Mississippi paddle steamer

Is it true?
Anchors are used to slow ships down.

NO. Anchors stop ships from floating away with the wind or tide. Anchors catch in rocks or sand on the seabed.

Amazing! Modern cruise liners are like huge floating hotels. There are cabins for thousands of passengers, restaurants, movie theaters, theaters, and a lot of swimming pools.

What was a steam liner?

A steam liner was a steam-powered passenger or cargo ship that crossed oceans on set routes at set times. In the 19th and 20th centuries, millions of people emigrated from Europe to North America on steam liners, taking their own food and bedding.

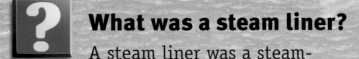

Club Med 1

Which modern liner has sails?

Cruise liners Club Med 1 (now called Wind Surf) and Club Med 2 have sails and an engine. Using the sails when the wind blows saves fuel.

RMS Queen Mary (launched 1934)

Tug

? **What does a tug do?**

A tug is a boat with very powerful engines that pulls or pushes large ships. Tugs help to move ships in and out of port. They also go to the rescue of broken-down ships, and tow them back to port to be repaired.

? What is the biggest ship?

Built in 1979, the oil tanker Knock Nevis is the biggest ship ever built. It is 1,504 feet long and 226 feet wide. Four soccer pitches would fit on its deck. Fully laden, it weighs 564,000 tons. In 2004 it was moored permanently in the Persian Gulf as a storage container.

? What is a ro-ro?

A ro-ro is a type of vehicle ferry. Ro-ro is short for roll-on, roll-off. It means that vehicles, such as cars, buses, and trucks, drive onto the ferry at one port and drive off again when the ferry arrives at its destination.

Is it true?
Some ships break ice.

YES. Ice breakers are ships that can break through thick ice. They help to keep routes open for other ships in the winter. An ice breaker has powerful engines and a very strong hull.

Container ship

Jahre Viking oil tanker

? What is a container ship?

A container ship is a cargo ship that carries metal boxes called containers. The containers are piled on its deck and sometimes in its hold, too. Each container carries a different sort of cargo.

55

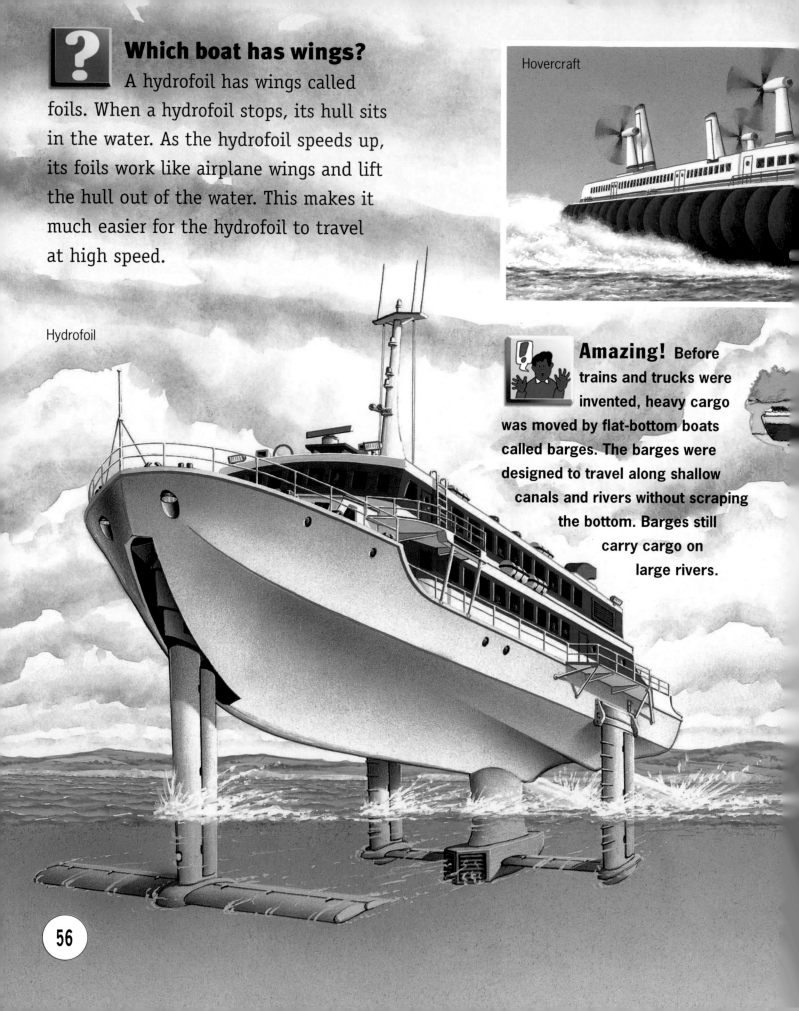

❓ Which boat has wings?

A hydrofoil has wings called foils. When a hydrofoil stops, its hull sits in the water. As the hydrofoil speeds up, its foils work like airplane wings and lift the hull out of the water. This makes it much easier for the hydrofoil to travel at high speed.

Hovercraft

Hydrofoil

Amazing! Before trains and trucks were invented, heavy cargo was moved by flat-bottom boats called barges. The barges were designed to travel along shallow canals and rivers without scraping the bottom. Barges still carry cargo on large rivers.

❓ Which boat flies?

A hovercraft is a boat that skims just above the water on a cushion of air. Huge fans blow air under the hovercraft. A rubber skirt holds the air in place. The hovercraft is moved along by propellers.

❓ Which ship has two hulls?

A ship or boat with two hulls is called a catamaran. Catamarans can travel more quickly than ships with one hull, which are called monohulls. High-speed ferries, such as the SeaCat, are catamarans. They have a top speed of more than 40 knots.

Is it true?
Some ships have three hulls.

YES. A ship with three hulls is called a trimaran. Most trimarans are sailing yachts. They have a large hull in the center and two small side hulls. When one small hull is in the water, the other is in the air.

SeaCat

? Who trawls the oceans?

Fishermen use boats called trawlers to catch fish and other sea creatures, such as shrimp. A trawler moves slowly through the water, pulling huge fishing nets behind. Every few hours the nets are pulled in and emptied. Trawlers have to be very strong and seaworthy because they often fish in stormy seas.

Shrimp trawler

? What is a factory ship?

A factory ship is a huge fishing ship where fish are prepared for market. The catch can even be frozen and stored on board. Factory ships sometimes catch their own fish, but normally they store fish caught by a whole fleet of much smaller fishing boats.

Factory ship

Whaling ship

? Who hunted whales?

Whalers were men who hunted whales for the oil in their blubber and also for their meat. When a whale was spotted, the whalers went after it in small boats and threw or fired spears, called harpoons, to kill it.

Amazing! Fishing boats called long liners catch fish on a fishing line up to 30 miles long. Hooks with bait are attached all the way along the line. Floats on the line have beacons that show where the line is in the dark.

✓✗ Is it true?
People go fishing in kayaks.

YES. Kayak is the proper name for a canoe with a deck on top and a small cockpit where the paddler sits. In the Arctic, Inuit fishermen hunt in kayaks made from wooden frames covered in seal skin.

? Which boats are unsinkable?

Lifeboats are rescue boats that don't sink even if they capsize (turn upside down). A lifeboat has a watertight cabin that makes it bob back upright. It has a strong hull and powerful engines for traveling quickly through rough seas.

Lifeboat

Amazing! The famous passenger liner Titanic was supposed to be unsinkable. But it sank on its maiden (first) voyage after hitting an iceberg in the North Atlantic Ocean in 1912.

60

Lightship

? What is a lightship?

A lightship is a ship with a lighthouse on its deck. Lightships are anchored near shallow water or dangerous rocks to warn sailors to keep clear. Most lightships have no crew because they are controlled automatically from shore.

Is it true?
Life savers row through surf to rescue people.

YES. Lifeguards row boats designed to break easily through surf near the beach. When they're off duty, lifeguards also race their boats.

Fire-fighting tug

? Which boat puts out fires?

Fire-fighting tugs are like fire engines at sea. They're designed to put out fires on ships, oil rigs, or in buildings on shore. They have powerful pumps that pump water from the sea to spray at fires.

61

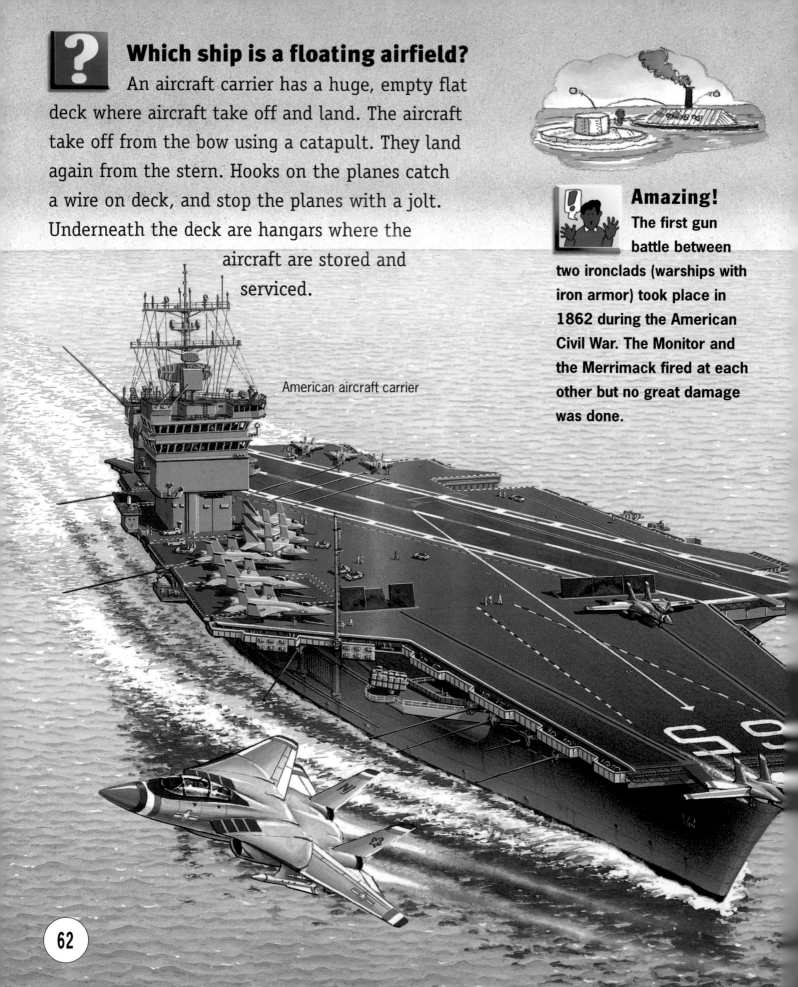

Which ship is a floating airfield?

An aircraft carrier has a huge, empty flat deck where aircraft take off and land. The aircraft take off from the bow using a catapult. They land again from the stern. Hooks on the planes catch a wire on deck, and stop the planes with a jolt. Underneath the deck are hangars where the aircraft are stored and serviced.

American aircraft carrier

Amazing!
The first gun battle between two ironclads (warships with iron armor) took place in 1862 during the American Civil War. The Monitor and the Merrimack fired at each other but no great damage was done.

❓ What was a pocket battleship?

Pocket battleships were small, fast German ships used in the 1930s. Only three of them were built. Each had six huge guns, armor more than 2 inches thick, and powerful diesel engines.

Admiral Graf Spee pocket battleship

Is it true?
Some ships are nuclear powered.

YES. Some large submarines, some aircraft carriers and some ice breakers have nuclear-powered engines. They can travel for several months without having to refuel.

❓ Which ship is invisible?

The United States Navy "stealth" warship doesn't show up clearly on enemy radar. Like the stealth aircraft, its special shape and paint scatter enemy radar signals, making it very difficult to detect.

Stealth warship

Is it true?
Most ships are jet powered.

NO. Most ships have diesel engines that turn their propellers. But some ships, such as high-speed ferries and warships, have turbines that work like aircraft jet engines.

Powerboats

? What is a yacht?

The word yacht normally means a sailing boat with a cabin below, or set into, the deck. People use yachts for cruising and for racing. The crew of a yacht has to "set" (adjust) the sails to make the best use of the wind. A small sailing boat without a cabin is called a dinghy.

Yachts

Which boats can travel the fastest?

The fastest boats are powerboats, with top speeds of about 150 mph (130 knots). Most powerboats are used for racing. They have huge outboard engines at the back and skim across the water's surface, bouncing against the waves and any trapped air beneath them.

Amazing! Some boats are pushed along by water jets. A powerful pump sucks in water from under the boat and squirts it out of the back. This shoots the boat forwards. Jet Skis also use water jets.

JANNINE · 31

25

Surfer

Who surfs across waves?

Surfers ride down the sloping faces of waves balanced on their boards. Expert surfers can stay on a wave all the way to shore. They often ride through the "tube" formed by the curling top of the wave.

65

? How big are submarines?

The biggest submarines are nuclear-powered naval submarines. The biggest of all are Russian Typhoon submarines. They're 564 feet long (as long as two soccer pitches) and weigh 50,000 tons. They can stay under water for months on end and sail around the world without refueling.

Turtle

World War II U-boat

Amazing! The first working submarine looked like a wooden barrel. It was built in 1776 and was called Turtle. The operator sat inside and pedaled to make its propellers turn. Turtle was designed to attack ships by diving under them and fixing a bomb to their hulls. But it was never successful.

? What was a U-boat?

U-boats were German submarines used in World War I and World War II. U-boat is short for underwater boat. U-boats sank thousands of ships. They crept up silently, hidden under the water, and fired missiles called torpedoes. The torpedoes zoomed through the water and exploded when they hit the ships.

YES. A submarine's sonar machine makes beeps of sound that spread out through the water. If the sound hits an object in the water, it bounces back to the submarine and is picked up by the sonar machine. The machine works out how big the object is and how far away it is.

Operating the periscope

What is a periscope?

Submarine crews use their periscopes to see ships on the surface above them when submarines are submerged. The top of the periscope sticks just above the surface. It works using several lenses and prisms (triangular pieces of glass).

What is a micro sub?

A micro sub (also called a submersible) is a small submarine, often used for exploring under the sea. The latest micro sub Deep Flight 1, launched in 1995, can dive to a depth of 3,300 feet.

Micro sub

Amazing!

Divers who repair undersea pipelines and oil rigs wear strong diving suits, like mini submersibles. They can dive to about 1,000 feet. The divers have to breathe oxygen mixed with helium, which gives them very squeaky voices!

Is it true?

Submarines can dive to the bottom of the ocean.

NO. The deepest a normal submarine can dive is about 2,300 feet. If a submarine went any deeper the huge water pressure would crush its hull and water would flood in.

Jason Junior

Alvin

? **What are Alvin and Jason Junior?**

Alvin is a submersible that carries a crew of three. Jason Junior is a robot submersible that can be operated from Alvin or from a ship on the surface. In 1985, Jason Junior discovered the wreck of the ocean liner Titanic at the bottom of the Atlantic Ocean.

? **How deep can submersibles go?**

Special, extra-strong-hulled submersibles called bathyscaphes can dive many miles under the sea. In 1960, the bathyscaphe Trieste made the deepest dive ever—an incredible 35,800 feet into the Marianas Trench in the Pacific Ocean.

Trieste

CHAPTER THREE

CARS

❓ What was a horseless carriage ?

A horseless carriage was a horse-drawn carriage with an engine in place of the horse. The first horseless carriages were powered by steam. In England, by the 1830s, some passenger services were operated with steam coaches. But the coaches were slow, noisy, and dirty, and wrecked the cart tracks!

James' steam carriage 1829

Daimler and his first car

❓ Who invented the first car?

Two German engineers, Karl Benz and Gottlieb Daimler, both built working cars in 1885. Each car had a small gas engine to drive it.

Amazing! When mechanical vehicles first appeared in Britain, a man had to walk in front of them carrying a red warning flag (or a red light at night). The Red Flag Law was introduced because other road users, such as horse riders, complained about the danger.

 ### Is it true?
The first cars didn't have steering wheels.

YES. The steering wheel did not appear on cars until the late 1890s. Before that, drivers steered with a lever, like the tiller on a boat, or by spinning handles on a small upright wheel on the end of a vertical pole.

? Which was the first car to be sold?

The first car to be sold was a three-wheel model built by Karl Benz. The first owner was a French engineer called Emile Roger, who bought his car in 1887. Soon Benz had a factory building cars for sale, but only a few of the three wheelers were sold.

Benz Patent-Motorwagen

In the early 1900s, there were no gas stations. Village blacksmiths often kept a supply of gas to sell to car drivers whose tanks had run dry. There were no garages or mechanics either, so drivers had to carry a tool kit and spare parts in their cars in case of a breakdown.

? Who got dressed up to go motoring?

Drivers and passengers of early cars had to dress up in protective clothes before driving into the countryside. Most cars had no windshield, doors, or bodywork to keep out wind and rain, or dust and mud from the dirt roads. So people wore thick fur coats or rubber capes, peaked hats, and enormous goggles over their eyes.

Model-T Ford

What was a "Tin Lizzie?"

The Model-T Ford was nicknamed "Tin Lizzie." It was small and reliable, and cheap enough for millions of people to buy.

Is it true?
Henry Ford invented the production line.

NO. Production lines existed before Henry Ford started making cars. But he did invent the moving line, where the cars moved along as parts were added.

Who spoke to the driver through a tube?

In some early cars, the passengers sat in the back behind a glass screen. The driver sat in the front. The passengers spoke to the driver through a metal tube to give him directions.

? Who drove a Silver Ghost?

The Silver Ghost was one of the first cars built by the Rolls-Royce company. Only rich people could afford to buy one, and they normally employed a chauffeur to drive it! Like all Rolls-Royce cars, the Silver Ghost was famous for being very quiet and extremely well made.

Austin Seven

? Which car was very cheap to run?

The Austin Seven was so economical that it used half a penny's worth of gas to travel a half mile. The Seven was so tiny that it was often called a "toy" car, but it was very cheap to buy.

Factory workers and their families used to go on days out to the seaside or to the city in a vehicle called a charabanc. A charabanc was like a wagon with benches in the back for passengers to sit on. The first charabancs were pulled by teams of horses.

 Is it true?

Taxis have always had meters.

YES. The word taxi is short for taximeter cab. A taximeter was a meter designed in 1891 that recorded the distance that a horse-drawn cab had traveled. When engine-powered taxis were introduced in 1907, they also had to have a meter.

Rolls–Royce Silver Ghost

Bugatti Royale

 Amazing! The Bugatti Type 41 Royale was designed by Ettore Bugatti to be the most luxurious car ever. His idea was that every royal family in Europe would buy one. The car was 22 feet long and had a 12-liter engine. But only six Royales were ever built, and only three were ever sold. Today, if a Bugatti Royale ever appears at auction, it fetches millions of dollars.

Amazing! In some early cars, passengers sat in the trunk. These "dickey seats" were hidden in the graceful, sloping tails of many early sports cars.

Who were the Bentley Boys?

Bentley Boys was the nickname of a group of drivers who raced Bentley cars in the late 1920s and early 1930s. Dark green Bentleys entered all the major races of the time, such as the endurance race at Le Mans.

Supercharged Bentley 4.5 liter

Is it true?
Drivers used hand signals before indicators were invented.

YES. Mechanical indicators weren't invented until 1932. Until then, drivers stuck their arms out of their cars to show which way they were going to turn. Flashing indicators appeared in the 1950s.

? What did the movie stars of the 1930s drive?

The stars of Hollywood movies of the 1930s bought luxury cars that they would look good in. They chose big, sporty convertibles so that their adoring fans could see them cruise by.

Auburn Speedster

? Who used fast cars to get away?

There were many gangs of criminals called gangsters in American cities in the 1930s. They used high-performance cars, such as the Ford V-8, to speed off after robbing banks or shooting at rival gangsters.

V-16 Cadillac 1930

What was the "Tin Goose?"

"Tin Goose" was the nickname of a short-lived rear-engined car called the Tucker '48. It had many original features, such as a strong passenger safety compartment and a third headlight, which swiveled as the driver turned the steering wheel.

Tucker's Tin Goose

Citroën Traction Avant

Why was the Citroën 7CV so special?

The Citroën 7CV of 1934 was the first popular car driven by its front wheels. It was known as the Traction Avant. It was also one of the first cars to have a one-piece body shell instead of a chassis with a body built on top.

Amazing! Even as late as 1931, some cars ran on steam power. Abner Doble built his first steam car in 1905, and went on to make several luxurious examples. They had plenty of power, and ran almost silently, but at prices between $8,000 and $11,000, they were beyond the reach of the average motorist.

❓ What was the people's car?

The people's car was the first Volkswagen (which means "people's car" in German). It was designed in the 1930s by Doctor Ferdinand Porsche to be a small family car that was cheap to run. It was soon nicknamed the Bug or Beetle. More than 21 million have been made.

Volkswagen Bug

Is it true?
Some cars have armor.

YES. An armored car is a military vehicle with steel plates on its body to make it bullet-proof. It usually has a small gun, too. Security companies often use vans with armor to transport valuable items or cash. Some limousines also have armor plating to make them bulletproof.

? Which car could really fly?

In 1949, American inventor Molt Taylor built a car that could be turned into an airplane. By 1953, the car had flown more than 25,000 miles. On the ground, the Aerocar towed its tail and wings in a trailer.

Airborne Aerocar

Aerocar without wings

Is it true?
American cars had the biggest fins of all.

YES. In the 1950s, American car designers began adding pointy parts, such as tail fins, to their cars. Some features were copied from the jet fighters of the time! Tail fins often had rows of lights up the back. These huge and thirsty cars also had plenty of chrome bodywork.

Amazing! The driver of a Cadillac Coupe de Ville did not have to worry about blinding other drivers with his or her headlights. The car had an electronic eye that detected headlights coming in the opposite direction and automatically dimmed its headlights.

? Which car had gull wings?

The doors on the 1952 Mercedes 300SL opened upward like a seagull's wings. The idea was given up because they couldn't be opened if the car turned over in an accident.

Mercedes gull wing

? What was a T-bird?

T-bird was the nickname given to the Ford Thunderbird. The first model appeared in 1954. It was a huge two-seater convertible. In the 1950s, American manufacturers built many huge gas guzzlers, such as the Thunderbird.

Ford Thunderbird

? Who drove around in a bubble?

The owners of small three-wheeled cars
made in the 1950s and 1960s drove in bubbles.
Their cars were nicknamed "bubble cars" because
of their round shape. The front of a bubble car
opened for the passengers to get in and out.

BMW Isetta bubble car

? What is a smart car?

The Smart car is a joint
venture between watchmakers Swatch
and Mercedes Benz. It's only 8 feet long,
and weighs 1,500 pounds. Its tiny size
makes it the ideal car in congested cities.

Smart car

84

Amazing! Some toy cars are much bigger than others! Wealthy parents can buy their children toy cars that are models of real cars. They have real engines, and the controls and lights of a real car. But they are not allowed on the road.

Morris Mini Minor

Is it true?
Cars can be stretched.

YES. A car is stretched by cutting it in two and adding an extra piece in the middle. The longest cars in the world are luxurious stretch limousines.

? What is a Mini?

The Mini is a tiny British car, which was designed by the famous car designer Alec Issigonis. It was launched in 1959, and became very fashionable in the 1960s. Many Minis were bought by movie actors and pop stars.

Who flames their cars?

Painting flames, which seem to flow along a car, is one of the oldest and most popular techniques used by people who customize their cars. Multicolored flames give the impression of speed and power. Customizing is a way of giving a car a character of its own by reshaping and repainting.

Lowrider

FLAMED

Is it true?

T-bucket is the name for a type of teacup.

NO. A T-bucket is a customized Model-T Ford with almost all of the original parts replaced with bigger, shinier, and more powerful parts, such as a huge engine, fat tires, improved suspension, and huge chrome exhaust pipes.

? What is a lowrider?

A lowrider is another type of customized car. These cars look as if they've been squashed. In fact, a section of the car above the doors is removed, and the suspension is lowered.

Flame-painted customized car

Street rod

 Amazing! Lowriders can jump in the air. The customized suspension fitted to these cars allows the body to be set at different heights. The suspension is so powerful that drivers can literally make their cars jump up and down.

? What is a street rod?

A street rod is an old family car, which its owner has customized for shows and displays. Street rods often have extra-powerful engines, a lowered roof, and huge rear tires. Really keen street-rod owners spend all their spare time keeping their cars shiny!

87

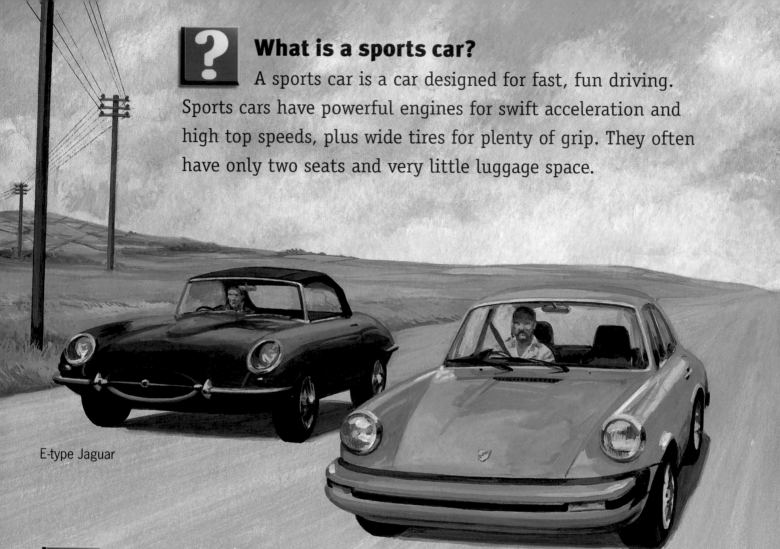

? What is a sports car?

A sports car is a car designed for fast, fun driving. Sports cars have powerful engines for swift acceleration and high top speeds, plus wide tires for plenty of grip. They often have only two seats and very little luggage space.

E-type Jaguar

Porsche 911

? Which sports car is still handmade?

Morgan sports cars are still hand built at their factory in Malvern, England. Although they look old fashioned, they can compete with any modern sports car.

Morgan Plus Eight

Amazing! The Austin-Healey Sprite sports car looked like a frog from the front! With its bulging headlights and cheerful smiling radiator grille, this popular classic soon earned the name "Frogeye" after its launch in 1958.

Is it true?

A drophead is a term for a car with a roof that drops off.

NO. Drophead is another word for convertible or cabriolet. The roof can be folded back either by hand, or with an electric motor. Roofless motoring is very popular in countries with a warm climate.

Lotus Elise

Ferrari 360 Modena

Which powerful car was named after a wild horse?

The Ford Mustang was named after the North American wild horse, or mustang. It was launched in 1964, and was a big hit because of its performance and low cost.

Ford Mustang

? What was Willys jeep?

Until the middle of World War II, Willys-Overland Company made ordinary cars. But they became famous for producing one of the best-known cars of all time. The Willys jeep was a four-wheel drive, general purpose (GP) vehicle, used by the American army.

Willys jeep

? What is four-wheel drive?

When a car has four-wheel drive, it means that the engine makes all four wheels turn. In most cars, the engine only turns two of the wheels. Four-wheel drive is excellent for traveling off-road on muddy tracks and up steep hills.

Amazing! King George V of England owned a six-wheeled limousine. It was built by Crossley in 1929, and had a 3.8-liter, six-cylinder engine. The king used it for cross country-expeditions, but it never went into production.

Is it true?

A car has been driven on the Moon.

YES. The missions Apollo 15, 16, and 17 that traveled to the Moon in the 1970s carried Lunar Roving Vehicles (LRVs) or Moon buggies. The astronauts drove the electric buggies around the Moon's surface, looking for interesting rocks. All three buggies are still on the Moon.

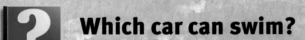

Which car can swim?

The 1962 Amphicar was part car, part boat. It had two propellers at the back, and the front wheels steered it, like a rudder. The large tail fins stopped water from flooding the engine.

Amphicar

How do robots make cars?

Factory robots weld and paint cars on production lines. They are instructed what to do by an engineer and then do it again and again very accurately. They work 24 hours a day and never get tired!

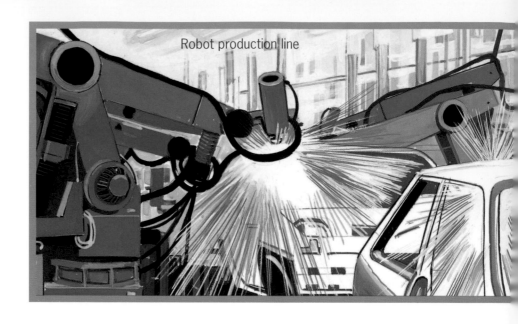

Robot production line

Who crash tests cars?

Crash-test dummies are artificial humans that sit inside cars as they're made to crash. The electronic dummies measure what happens to them, and if the cars' safety features work properly. Cars that fail the tests have to be redesigned.

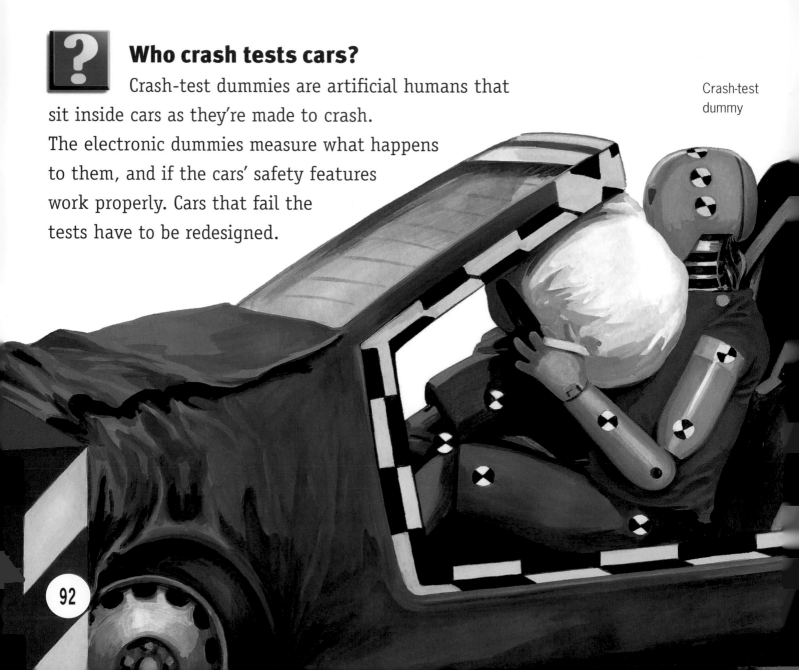

Crash-test dummy

Is it true?

Cars are tested in wind tunnels.

YES. A wind tunnel is a tube with a huge fan at one end. Engineers check how air flows around the cars. The easier it flows, the faster the car can go and the less fuel it uses.

Amazing! When cars wear out they're crushed into tiny cubes by a huge machine. It squashes the car first one way and then the other. The metal in the cube is recycled to make new cars.

How are cars designed?

Every part of a car is designed using computers. Engineers draw what the parts and the car will look like, and the computer helps to control the machines that make the parts.

1 Fuel and air are drawn into the cylinder.

2 Fuel-air mixture is squeezed by the piston.

3 The mixture is ignited by a spark, which forces the piston down.

4 The piston forces the exhaust gases out.

? What is an internal combustion engine?

An internal combustion engine is the type of engine that most cars have. "Internal combustion" means that a fuel and air mixture burns inside can-shaped cylinders inside the engine.

Engine

Brakes

Suspension

Tire with tread

❓ Why do cars have gears?

Cars have gears so that they can start off and move at different speeds. In a manual car, first gear is for starting off. First and second gears are for going slowly. Fourth and fifth gears are for going quickly.

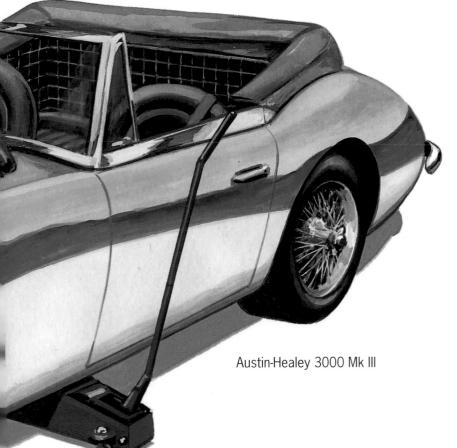

Austin-Healey 3000 Mk III

Is it true?
The tread of a tire grips the road.

NO. The rubber of the tires grips the road. Tread is the pattern of grooves around the outside of a tire. The grooves let water escape from between a tire and a wet road so that the rubber can touch the road surface for grip.

❓ What are springs and shock absorbers?

Springs and shock absorbers make up a car's suspension, which gives the people inside a smooth ride. Springs let the car's wheels move up and down as it goes over bumps. Shock absorbers stop the car from bouncing after it's passed over the bumps.

Which car had an ejector seat?

In the movie Goldfinger, James Bond drove an Aston Martin DB5 with a passenger ejector seat. Bond used it to get rid of one of his enemies. The Aston Martin also had machine guns, armor, and spikes that came out of the wheels to slash the tires of other cars.

Aston Martin DB5

BMT 214A

Amazing! When the Pope travels away from the Vatican, he takes a special car, nicknamed the "Popemobile." The car has a bulletproof glass dome. When the Pope goes on tours, he stands under the dome holding onto a hand rail. His followers can easily see him, and he can see them, without the risk of attack.

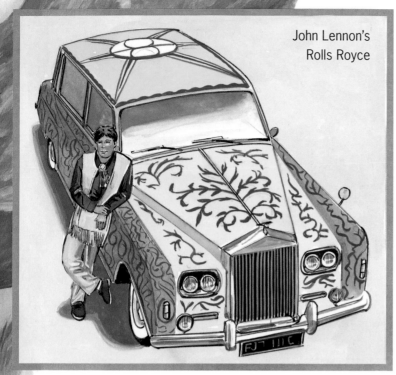
John Lennon's
Rolls Royce

**Who had his
Rolls–Royce painted
in amazing flowery patterns?**

The Beatles were the world's biggest
pop group in the 1960s. Singer John
Lennon painted his Rolls-Royce
Phantom VI with trendy colorful
patterns.

**? Which supercar had
six wheels?**

The wedge-shape Panther Six was designed
by Bob Jankel in 1977. It was more than
16 feet long, and over 6.5 feet wide. Both
pairs of front wheels steered the car, which
was never sold to the public.

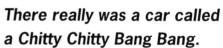

Is it true?
*There really was a car called
a Chitty Chitty Bang Bang.*

YES. Ian Flemming, writer of the
children's novel Chitty Chitty Bang Bang,
named his fictional flying car for a real
racing car built by Count Louis
Zborowski in the early 1920s.

Panther Six

97

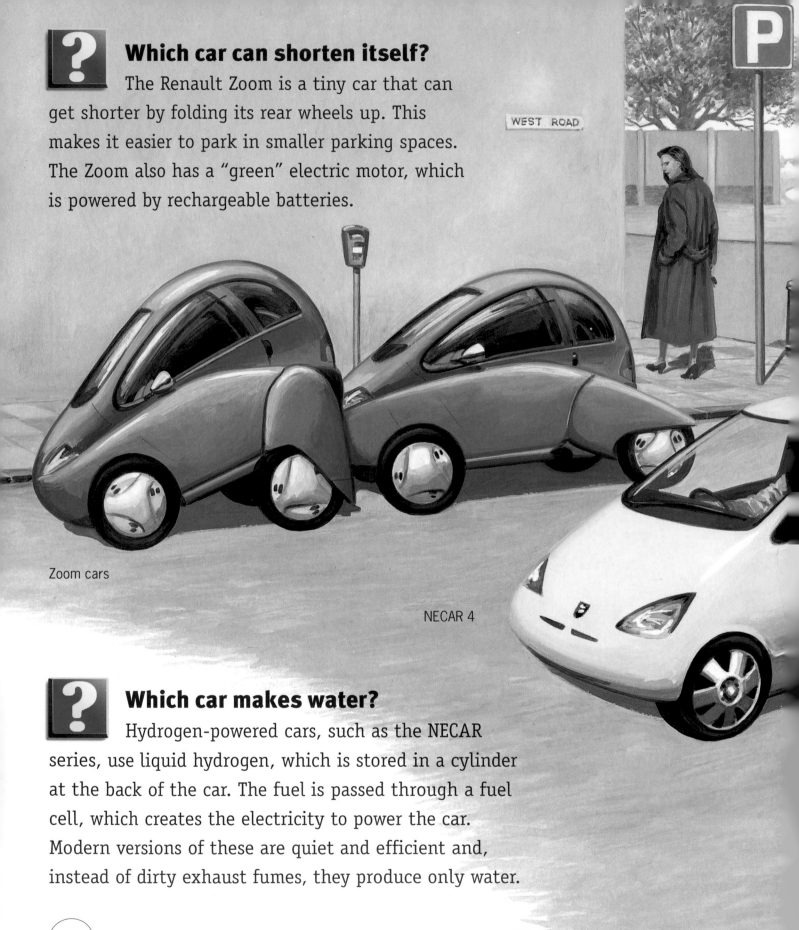

❓ Which car can shorten itself?

The Renault Zoom is a tiny car that can get shorter by folding its rear wheels up. This makes it easier to park in smaller parking spaces. The Zoom also has a "green" electric motor, which is powered by rechargeable batteries.

WEST ROAD

Zoom cars

NECAR 4

❓ Which car makes water?

Hydrogen-powered cars, such as the NECAR series, use liquid hydrogen, which is stored in a cylinder at the back of the car. The fuel is passed through a fuel cell, which creates the electricity to power the car. Modern versions of these are quiet and efficient and, instead of dirty exhaust fumes, they produce only water.

YES. In Brazil, there's an alternative source of fuel taken directly from a plant. One "petrol tree" is able to produce about 5 gallons of fuel. The Brazilians grow huge plantations of these trees to help the problem of increasing fuel shortages.

? Which car runs on sunlight?

Cars are being developed that can convert sunlight into electricity to power their engines. The solar-powered car of the future might look like the vehicle pictured below, with solar panels on the roof.

Prototype solar car

ecar 4

CHAPTER FOUR

TRAINS

❓ Which train was pulled by horses?

Between 1800 and 1825, there were "trains" without engines in Wales and Austria. Horses pulled carriages along the rails. It was a smoother ride than road travel.

❓ Which train was the first to carry passengers?

Stephenson's Locomotion was the first engine to be used on a public railroad, the Stockton and Darlington, England, in 1825. Stephenson's Rocket won a large cash prize in a competition four years later.

Locomotion

? What was the first train engine?

Richard Trevithick, a mine engineer, first demonstrated a mobile engine on rails in 1804. It pulled 70 men and 10 tons of iron ore, in front of a crowd of amazed onlookers. His next engine became a fairground ride.

Trevithick's Catch Me Who Can, 1808

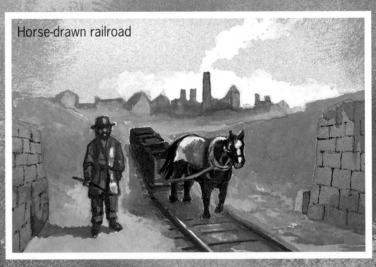

Horse-drawn railroad

 Amazing! There were horse-drawn trains 50 years ago! The Fintona Branch of Ireland's Great Northern railroad remained horse-powered until the early 1950s.

Is it true?

The ancient Greeks had a steam engine!

YES. Hero of Alexander wrote about a steam-powered spinning ball, called the "aeolipile" in 200 B.C. But since slave labor was free, no one bothered to use the engine as a labor-saving device.

Couplings

Trains use special links called couplings to clip different parts together. Trains used to be coupled by hand, which could be dangerous.

What's a locomotive?

A locomotive is the part of the train that contains the engine. It does the work of pulling (or pushing) the train along the track. Locomotives may have to carry their fuel with them. They have special wheels to grip the track.

American Baldwin locomotive

Who steers the train?

Trains follow the track they're on, so they don't need a steering wheel. A person in the junction box can change the direction of a train by moving special junctions in the track called points.

Junction box

Amazing! Some trains lean over! Modern fast trains take corners so quickly that passengers might slosh around inside. Computers in the train "feel" the sideways forces, and tilt the train in the other direction so that you don't spill your drink.

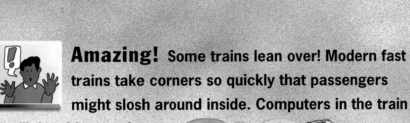

Is it true?
Some trains are blown along by the wind.

YES. At least, some were, especially when fuel was hard to find. America's Baltimore & Ohio railroad experimented with sail power in the 1830s.

Boiler

Smoke stack

Piston

 How is the steam made?

Steam trains all need a fireperson, who shovels coal, or similar fuel, into a firebox. The heat of the fire boils the water, which turns to steam. Smoke from the fire puffs out of the funnel on the smoke stack.

How does steam power work?

A steam engine is like a big kettle. It uses the pressure of steam to push against pistons inside cylinders. The pistons move sliding rods called linkages, which turn the wheels and make the train move.

Russian royal railroad, 1837

 Amazing! Russia's first railroad was just for royal vacations! The Czar of Russia had three locomotives made for him in 1837. They ran on a private line from his palace to a royal resort.

YES. In 1938, a steam engine called Mallard reached 126 mph, while pulling a 240-ton train. That's still a record for a steam engine. It had been souped-up by Herbert Gresley, doubling its power. Mallard is now in a museum in York, England.

❓ When was steam power used?

The golden age of steam was from about 1850, until as late as 1950. Since then, steam trains have disappeared from industrial countries, where they only survive as tourist attractions. Steam locomotives still do most of the hard work in many developing countries.

Patrick Stirling's Single locomotive

Which diesel was a "centipede?"

America's Pennsylvania
Railroad used Baldwin diesel engines
in pairs. Each one had 12 small
wheels on each side. Linked together,
making a 6,000 horse-power monster,
they looked like they had 24 "legs."

1924 Kitson-Still

Amazing! Diesel engines can
be steam engines, too. The 1924
Kitson-Still used a diesel engine for
its main power, but also used the heat of the
engine to create steam. This powered an extra
set of drive wheels.

Why did diesel take over from steam?

Diesel power first came into use to cope with
the problem of smoke in cities and underground railroads.
During World War II, military diesel engines became
lighter and smaller. Just like today's trains,
the engines fitted under the floors
of the carriages.

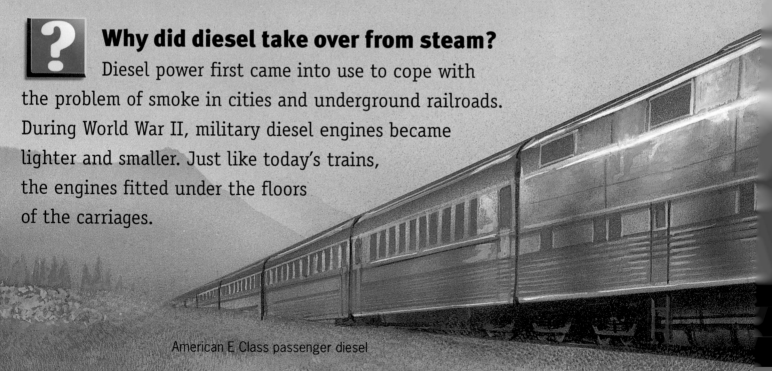

American E Class passenger diesel

Which diesel looked like an airplane?

The German Kruckenburg of 1931 had a huge propeller at the back, which pushed it along like an airplane on rails. It reached speeds up to 142 mph during a 6-mile speed trial. Unfortunately, it was too noisy and dangerous for everyday use.

1931 Kruckenburg

Is it true?
Diesel engines use electric motors.

YES. Many diesel-engined trains actually use electric motors to turn the wheels. The engine itself uses diesel fuel. It turns a generator, which creates the electricity needed by the electric motors. This is because electric motors turn powerfully at all speeds, unlike a diesel engine.

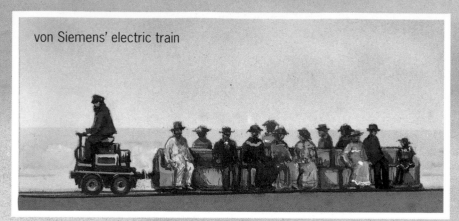

von Siemens' electric train

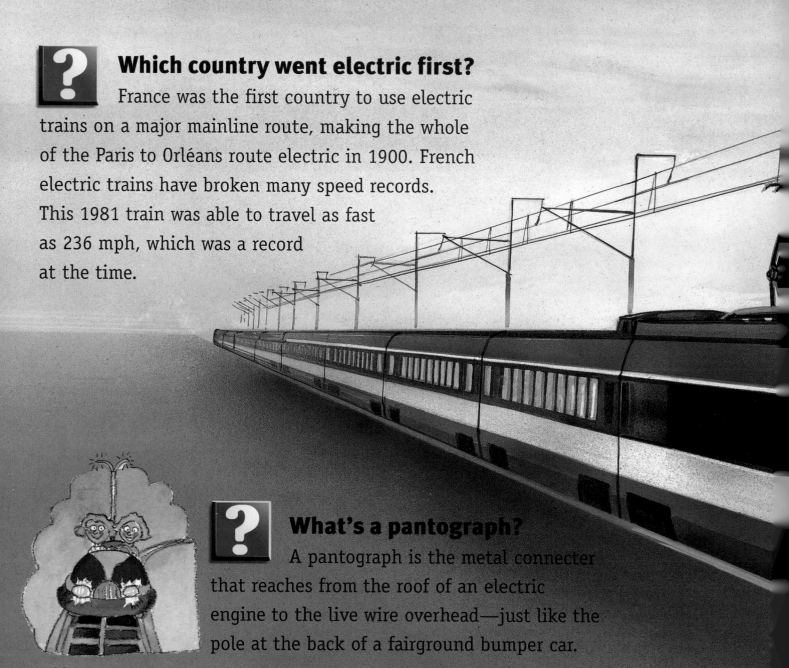

? Which country went electric first?

France was the first country to use electric trains on a major mainline route, making the whole of the Paris to Orléans route electric in 1900. French electric trains have broken many speed records. This 1981 train was able to travel as fast as 236 mph, which was a record at the time.

? What's a pantograph?

A pantograph is the metal connecter that reaches from the roof of an electric engine to the live wire overhead—just like the pole at the back of a fairground bumper car.

Amazing! Some electric trains travel all over Europe. In the 1970s, Trans-Europ-Express was designed to use the different electricity supplies in different European countries. In the 1980s, EuroCity trains took over the routes.

Underground train

? Are electric engines better than diesel?

Electric power lets trains use energy without creating too much mess. The only pollution is at the power station where the electricity is made. Electric power is ideal for trams and underground trains in cities. Diesels are better on long routes where great lengths of electrical cables and wires would be too expensive.

French TGV high-speed train, 1981

SNCF

British Rail coal train

❓ What is a chaldron?

Coal wagons are also called chaldrons. They are loaded at the mine, then travel to the nearest port for loading onto boats, or to a power station. Chaldrons are emptied by tipping them over, or by opening a trapdoor below.

❓ Which train was the most luxurious?

The Orient Express offered passengers a lounge, a ladies' drawing room, fully serviced bedroom suites, and a fantastic dining room. Diners ate in evening dress. A modern version of the Orient Express still runs between London and Venice.

Dining car in the Orient Express

Amazing! Until the invention of the air brake in 1869, brakemen had to run along the train applying brakes in every car, one by one! Today the brakes are worked by the driver.

What's a Pullman?

George Pullman was a carpenter who repaired two worn passenger carriages in Chicago in 1859. By the 1920s, the Pullman company had 10,000 luxurious Pullman cars in service. They became famous for the comfort, style, and excellent service offered to their lucky passengers.

Mail train

Is it true?
There are post offices on wheels.

YES. There are underground and overground mail trains in parts of the world. Some don't stop—instead, bags of mail are caught or dropped off as the train whizzes past. Sorters in the train work very quickly in case any of the collected mail has to go to the next station!

Alpine rack-and-pinion railroad

Who rode on a wooden track?

A four mile track in Tasmania was made of gum tree wood! Convicts pushed carts up a hill, then jumped aboard for the downhill ride.

Amazing! Some trains have teeth! On steep hills smooth track is too slippery. Trains would slip going up and slide on the way down! Rack-and-pinion tracks have a third, toothed rail for trains to grip with a special cog, or "tooth," on the wheel.

How are tracks laid?

First, the ground must be prepared. This might mean clearing woodland, or cutting a flat route through hilly land. Wooden "sleepers" are laid at exact distances from each other, and the metal rails are then attached to them. As the track gets longer, supply trains travel along it, delivering more sleepers and rails.

Sleeper

Is it true?
All train tracks have two rails.

NO. Monorails have just one. Monorail trains are important parts of the transport system in many big cities. Monorail systems are often found in amusement parks, airports, and large industrial sites.

Which train was pushed by air?

In 1861, a train was built that was pushed through a tunnel by a blast of air. The tunnel was only 30 inches wide, and the experimental train was designed to carry mail bags.

Monorail

Laying track in Canada, 1880

San Francisco cable car

? Which trains travel by cables?

Cable cars, such as the ones in San Francisco, are pulled along by a moving loop of cable, made from strong steel. The cable passes through a slot between the rails, and the cars are secured onto it. This way, cable cars can climb very steep hills.

? Where is the longest straight?

It's difficult to build straight stretches of track near towns, but much easier in empty parts of the world. The longest stretch of straight track is in the desert of Australia. It is perfectly straight for 297 miles.

 Amazing! Railroads can go missing! During the American Civil War, the South ripped up some of its less important railroads to use as spare parts along the battle front. Florida and Texas gave up their entire networks!

YES. If all the train tracks in the United States were laid end-to-end, they would form a single track that would go almost six times around the world—that's 150,000 miles!

? Can trains travel the length of Africa?

There is no direct link from Cairo in North Africa to Cape Town, South Africa, 6,050 miles away. The Briton Cecil Rhodes tried to build a railroad line in the late 19th century, but one of his problems was finding enough workmen—28 of his men were eaten by lions on the Athi Plains in Kenya! However, there are plans to complete this link soon.

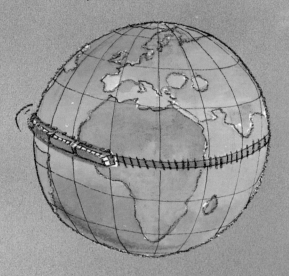

Australian Indian Pacific railway

Tunnel-boring machine

❓ Is the Channel Tunnel longest?

No. The Channel Tunnel, between England and France, is 31 miles in total. The Seikan, Japan's tunnel between the main islands of Honshu and Hokkaido, travels an amazing 33.5 miles underground.

Royal Albert Bridge, spanning the River Tamar, England

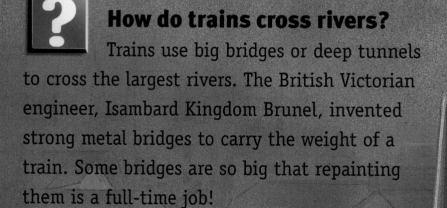

❓ How do trains cross rivers?

Trains use big bridges or deep tunnels to cross the largest rivers. The British Victorian engineer, Isambard Kingdom Brunel, invented strong metal bridges to carry the weight of a train. Some bridges are so big that repainting them is a full-time job!

Where was the first raised city railroad?

New York City had a serious traffic problem in the 1880s, and that was before cars! An "Elevated Railroad," known as "the L" for short, was built above the streets. It still works today.

New York Elevated Railway

Amazing! You can take a train on a boat. Train ferries started operating in the late 1800s between England and France. Passengers stayed in their seats all the way from London to Paris!

Is it true?
Box Hill tunnel knows its creator's birthday.

YES. Brunel built it at a special angle. Each year, only on his birthday, the sun shines right through the entire two-mile tunnel in southern England.

I.K.BRUNEL

Who slept in the "Tube?"

During World War II, when London was being severely bombed, many people sheltered in Underground, or Tube, stations. It must have been a real squeeze, but it was much safer than staying above ground.

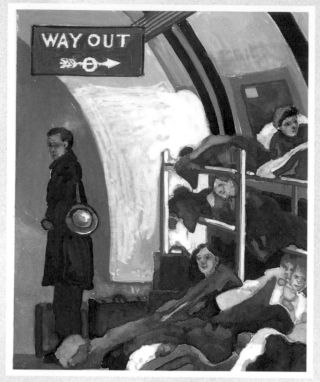

London Underground, 1940

When were trains first used in war?

Trains were used in the American Civil War, between 1861 and 1865. But World War I relied even more on trains to bring huge numbers of soldiers to the battle lines in northern Europe.

Amazing! General Sherman used rails for hairpins. In the American Civil War, the North broke up southern railroads, bending the rails around posts, to make "hairpins," to stop them being reused.

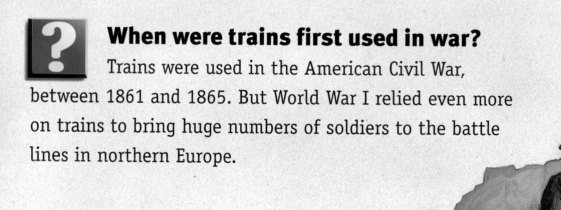

Is it true?

The first tanks traveled by train.

YES. In World War I, secret new tanks were wrapped up and shipped to battle by train. Everyone was told the bundles were oil tanks, and the name stuck!

Armored train, South Africa, 1900

? What train is a tank?

Some trains were armored to protect important generals as they traveled around with orders for their troops. Some armored trains even had cannons onboard!

World War I troop transporter

What was the biggest train crime?

In 1963, a train was robbed in Buckinghamshire, England. The thieves got away with used bills worth millions of dollars, a huge sum of money even today.

Scene of the Great Train Robbery

 Amazing! Trains at Mwatate Dam, in Kenya, have to slow down for demons. The villagers nearby thought that trains were having a lot of accidents there because the local spirits were angry. Trains began pausing briefly to salute the spirits, and there hasn't been a crash since!

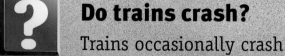 **Do trains crash?**
Trains occasionally crash for a number of reasons—there might be a points failure, or a weak bridge. Amazingly, no one was killed when this cattle train crashed through the front of an Irish railroad station. Rail travel is usually very safe though.

Train crash, Harcourt Street Station, Dublin

Did railroad projects always work?

No. The English almost built a Channel Tunnel in 1883. They tunneled over a mile under the sea, but the government was worried the French would use the tunnel to invade England, so it was abandoned!

 Is it true?
Some trains are too big.

YES. The Soviet Union made a locomotive in 1934 that was too long. Its nonswiveling wheels and heavy weight actually straightened out curves in the track, leaving it stuck in a ditch!

Derailment, Russia 1934

Amazing! Queen Victoria's bridge could have killed her. A train line to her castle at Balmoral, Scotland, bridging the Tay estuary, blew down in 1879, killing as many as 90 passengers on a northbound train.

Tay Bridge disaster

 ### Can any trains travel upside down?

Roller coasters are a type of train. They have wheels on the rail, beside the rail, and under the rail, so they can't fall off. Some roller coasters make the most of this safety feature, and turn upside down. Eek!

Miniature railroad

 Is it true?
You can ride a toy train.

YES. But only some of them! Model makers can make real steam trains five or six times smaller than the real thing.

 ## Which train can climb a volcano?

Aso Boy, a replica of an American Wild West steam engine, takes tourists in Japan to the summit of Mount Aso, a huge volcanic crater. The engine was built in 1922, and its line is 37 miles long.

Do toy trains ever crash?

After some famous train crashes at the start of the 20th century, children with train sets often staged big crashes. For extra effect, a German toymaker created a special spring-loaded toy train that "exploded" on impact.

Roller coaster

How long is the longest train?

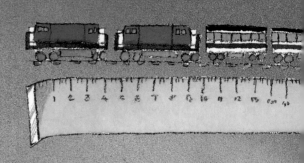

The longest train ever was a freight train measuring 4.5 miles! The longest passenger train was a measly 1,895 yards, but the Belgian railroad couldn't find a platform long enough to park it!

Modern TGV

Laying track

Amazing! Eight men can lay 10 miles of track in a day! A team of eight track layers in the United States set this world record on April 18, 1869.

Which train is fastest?

France pioneered fast trains after World War II. When Japan introduced the Shinkansen "bullet train" in the 1960s, France responded with the TGV. An experimental TGV has reached 356 mph!

Is it true?
A train can weigh more than the Eiffel Tower.

YES. An Australian mine train was weighed in 1996 at 72,191 tons—that's more than eight Eiffel Towers!

Trans-Siberian Express

Which train travels farthest?

The once-weekly service between Moscow, Russia, and Pyongyang, North Korea, travels 6,346 miles, taking almost eight days. Part of its route is also traveled by the Trans-Siberian Express, or The Russia. This train has featured in several books and movies. It is second only in fame to the Orient Express.

Which train flies?

Really fast future trains might not bother with wheels. They could ride on a cushion of air, like a hovercraft. The nose of the train squashes air underneath its belly as it jets along, and the squashed air lifts it above the ground. The Aerotrain already exists as an experimental vehicle.

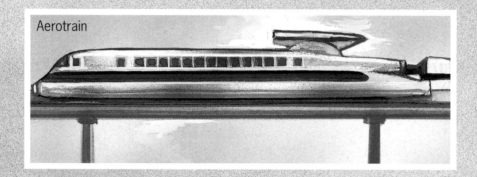
Aerotrain

 Amazing! One sled traveled at Mach 8. An unmanned rocket vehicle on rails achieved 6,121 mph in an American experiment in 1982. On straight track, it could make the eight-day Trans-Siberian trip in less than one hour!

What is a bullet train?

Japan's fastest trains, the Shinkansen, were nicknamed bullet trains because of their pointy noses—and high speed! The fastest, the N700 series, travel at 186 mph. With no time wasted at airports, traveling by bullet train can be quicker than flying by jet!

Are trains "green?"

Trains are less harmful to the environment than most other kinds of transport. They are particularly important in cities, where underground trains, trams, and monorails can reduce pollution from cars, buses, and taxis. For long-distance journeys, trains use much less fuel than jet aircraft.

Is it true?

Some trains run on magnets.

YES. Maglev trains use repelling magnets to float above the track. The track doesn't wear out, and the trains can slip along at amazing speeds. China's Shanghai Maglev runs from the city to the airport at 250 mph!

JR500 Shinkansen bullet train

CHAPTER FIVE

MOTORCYCLES

Who was the first to put pedals on a bike?

In 1838, a Scottish blacksmith called Kirkpatrick Macmillan built the first bike with pedals. Before this, bike riders kicked the ground to move along.

Kirkpatrick Macmillan

Penny farthing

What was a penny farthing?

A penny farthing was a bike of the 1870s, named after two British coins. It had an enormous front wheel (the penny) and a small rear wheel (the farthing).

Amazing! In the 1880s, couples often rode side by side on tricycles (bikes with three wheels) called sociables. Each person had a set of pedals, which turned the huge rear wheels.

132

? What was a safety bicycle?

The safety bicycle was the first bike to look like today's bikes. It appeared in 1885. It had two wheels the same size, a diamond-shape metal frame, pedals that turned the rear wheel using a chain, and brakes worked by levers on the handlebars.

 Is it true?
People raced tricycles.

YES. In the 1880s, the tricycle was not just a bike for children, as it is today. It was popular with adults, too. Tricycle racing was one of the first forms of bike racing. Race events were held on bumpy streets and wooden tracks.

Safety bicycle

133

❓ What is a driveshaft?

A driveshaft is a rod that carries power from a bike's engine to its rear wheel. Some early bikes, such as the Belgian FN of 1906, had driveshafts instead of belts or chains. The shaft turned the wheel using gears.

FN 1906

❗ Amazing! In the early 1900s, women always wore dresses, even when they rode on motorcycles. So some bikes had a dress guard made of string, which stopped dresses from getting tangled in the engine or rear wheel.

❓ What were leather belts for?

Most motorcycles today use a chain to drive the rear wheel. But many motorcycles made before 1910 used a thick leather belt instead. Belts were unreliable, because they wore out quickly, often broke, and even slipped in the rain!

? When was a drive chain first used?

Most modern bikes have a flexible metal chain, which carries power from the engine to the rear wheel. Drive chains were introduced on some bikes in the early 1900s, such as the 1905 Scott. Chains are made up of dozens of short pieces linked together.

Two-stroke Scott 1905

Douglas 1911

Is it true?
Belt drives are still used today.

YES. Most modern bikes use a drive chain, but some have belts instead. The belts are made from rubber, strengthened with fabric. Belts are lighter than chains and need less maintenance. A few modern bikes have driveshafts instead of a chain or belt.

? Who were Harley and Davidson?

William, Walter, and Arthur Davidson, along with William Harley, founded Harley-Davidson in 1903. Their first bike went into production in 1905, with their first factory in 1906.

1912 Harley-Davidson

Amazing! The Italian company Moto Guzzi, founded in the 1920s, borrowed the eagle-shape badge of the Italian Air Force to put on their bikes.

RK4907

1930 Brough Superior

1928 Indian 101 Scout

? Why was Brough superior?

British engineer George Brough designed one of the best and most expensive bikes of all time, and called it the Brough Superior. It was known as the "Rolls-Royce of motorcycles." The most famous owner of a Brough Superior was the British war hero Lawrence of Arabia.

What was an Indian?

Indian was a famous American company that manufactured motorcycles in the first half of the 20th century. One of Indian's most successful bikes was the Indian Scout, which appeared in 1920 and was manufactured for 30 years. It had a 600 cc engine, driveshaft, and a top speed of 75 mph.

Is it true?

Rollie Free rode a Vincent Black Shadow in a swimsuit.

YES. The Vincent Black Shadow was the first motorcycle to reach over 150 mph. It did it in 1948, and its rider, Rollie Free, wore just a swimsuit and rode lying flat to reduce air drag. If he had sat upright on the saddle, he wouldn't have reached this speed.

Where is a motorcycle's engine located?

A motorcycle's engine is between the two wheels, attached to the bike's frame. Above the engine, just in front of the driver's seat, is the fuel tank. Exhaust pipes carry waste gases from the engine to the rear of the bike.

Fuel tank

Exhaust pipes

Cylinder head

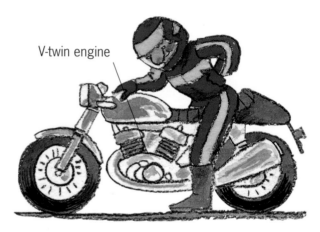

V-twin engine

Are motorcycle engines all the same shape?

The shape of an engine depends on how many cylinders it has and how they are arranged. A V-twin engine has two cylinders in a V shape. A straight-four has four cylinders in a line.

Amazing! U.S. company Boss Hoss makes limited production motorcycles with engines larger than 8,000 cc—four times larger than a family car engine.

The Yamaha 1600cc has a 1,600 cc engine.

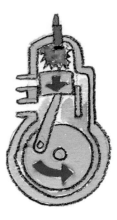

Spark plug ignites fuel-air mixture

Fuel and air explode

Exhaust gases are released

Piston moves down

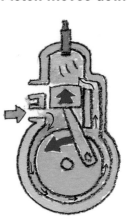

Fuel-air mixture enters cylinder

Piston moves up

Fuel-air mixture is compressed

Piston

? What is a two-stroke engine?

A two-stroke engine is a simple gasoline engine often used on small motorbikes, mopeds, and scooters. Larger motorcycles have a four-stroke gasoline engine. Two-stroke engines use more fuel and make more pollution.

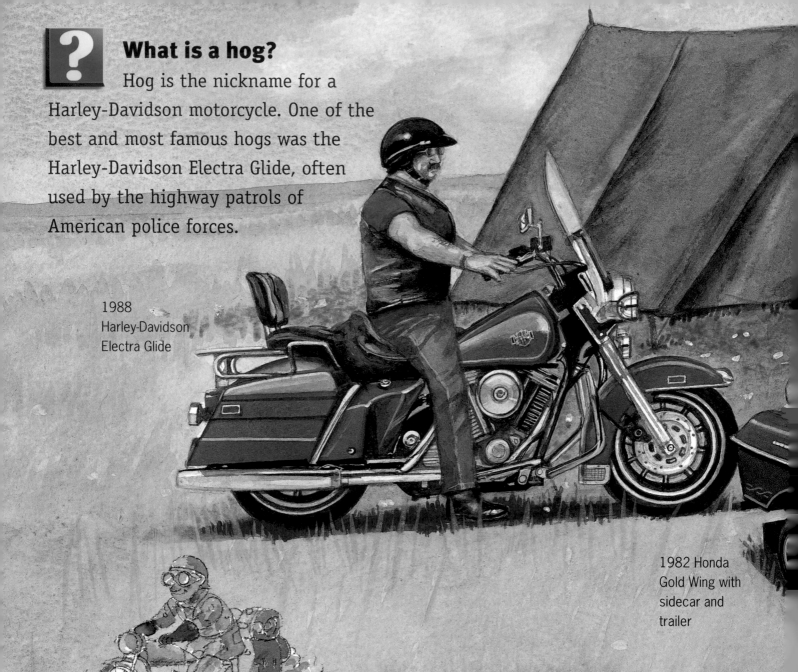

❓ What is a hog?

Hog is the nickname for a Harley-Davidson motorcycle. One of the best and most famous hogs was the Harley-Davidson Electra Glide, often used by the highway patrols of American police forces.

1988
Harley-Davidson
Electra Glide

1982 Honda
Gold Wing with
sidecar and
trailer

Amazing! Carl Stevens Clancy rode around the world on a motorcycle in 1912, the first person to achieve this feat. His 18,000-mile journey started in the United States, and took him through Europe, Africa, Japan, and back home to New York.

❓ What is a sidecar?

A sidecar is a small one-wheeled car that bolts onto the side of a motorcycle. It turns the motorcycle into a three-wheeled vehicle. The sidecar can carry a passenger or luggage. With a sidecar attached, the bike rider cannot lean over on corners.

142

What is a Gold Wing?

A Gold Wing is a giant touring bike made by the Japanese company Honda. The Gold Wing is very smooth to ride, has a seat for a passenger, and an engine powerful enough to pull a sidecar and a trailer. It's perfect for long-distance touring.

Is it true?
Passengers used to ride in baskets.

YES. The bodies of sidecars for early motorcycles were made of wicker, which was also used to make baskets. Wicker is made by weaving bendable wooden branches together.

? What is a scooter?

A scooter has small wheels, a small engine near the rear wheel, and a gap in the frame for the rider's legs. They are cheap to run and good for getting about in busy towns.

Amazing! You can buy toy motorcycles that are models of real bikes, with tiny engines and the same controls as a full-size bike. However, they're not allowed on the highway.

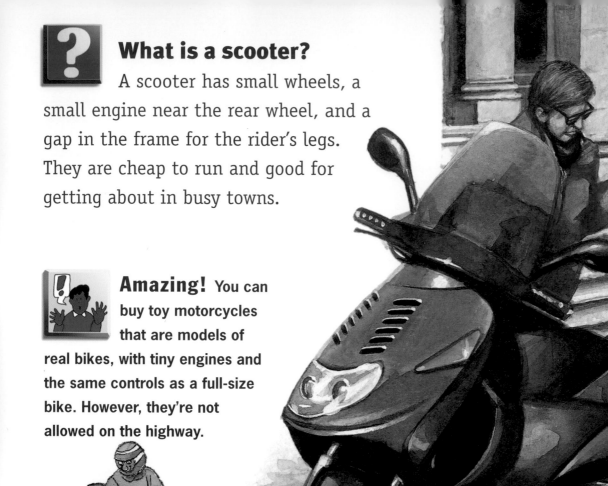

Italjet Millennium 125

? Which is the best-selling motorcycle ever?

The 50 cc Honda Super Cub, which went on sale in 1958, is the biggest selling motorcycle ever. This little bike is cheap to run, and is still popular all over the world.

Is it true?
The scooter is a recent invention.

NO. Scooters became popular in Italy in the 1950s, and in the 1960s they became very trendy. They were ridden by young British men called mods, who dressed in green parka coats and customized their scooters with a lot of mirrors and flags.

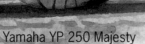
Yamaha YP 250 Majesty

? Which scooter fits in a car trunk?

The American-made Autoped, which was produced in 1915, could be folded up to fit into the trunk of a car. In recent years, as traffic has become busier, fold-up scooters have become popular again for cheap and speedy travel.

21st-century scooter

145

Amazing!
Trials bikes can make short hops up almost vertical rock faces. The rider needs good balance and expert control of the clutch and gears.

? Which motorcyclists wear armor?

Riders in motocross races wear tough, plastic body armor to protect them in case they fall off, or are hit by other bikes. They also wear long, tough boots, helmets, and goggles to keep mud out of their eyes.

? What is a trials bike?

Trials bikes are designed for riding on steep, rough, and rocky ground. They are ridden in motorbike trials, where riders have to ride over obstacles without stopping or putting their feet down to balance.

Trials bike

Is it true?

No one has crossed the desert on a motorbike.

NO. Riders often take part in motocross competitions held in deserts. There are also long-distance desert motorbike rallies, such as the Dakar Rally, which crosses the dusty Sahara.

Dakar Rally, from Paris to Dakar in Senegal

Motocross

Which bikes have knobbly tires?

Trials bikes and motocross bikes have tires with a deep, knobbly tread around the outside. The tread helps the tires to grip the wet and muddy ground during competitions.

1942 Harley-Davidson WLA

? Who had a holster on a Harley?

U.S. Army despatch riders of World War II carried a rifle in a holster on their Harley-Davidson WLA 45 motorcycles. More than 80,000 WLAs were made during the war, and many of them were bought by ex-soldiers afterward.

Is it true?

The first U.S. soldier to enter Germany after World War I rode a Harley?

YES. Corporal Holtz, an American soldier, was photographed riding into Germany on a Harley with a sidecar, the day after the war ended in 1918.

Who dropped from the sky with mini bikes?

During World War II, when some Allied and German soldiers jumped from their aircraft, their mini motorcycles parachuted down with them.

German mini-scooter

 Amazing! In World War II the German army used a vehicle called a Ketten Kraftrad that was half motorcycle, half armored car. It had a motorcycle front wheel and caterpillar tracks.

Who had machine guns on their motorcycles?

German World War II soldiers rode high-speed BMW motorcycles with sidecars. One soldier operated the heavy machine gun in the sidecar.

BMW R-75

? What is a TT race?

TT races are held every year on the public streets of the Isle of Man, part of the British Isles. TT stands for Tourist Trophy because, when the races started in 1907, they were for touring motorcycles.

Norton Isle of Man TT racer

1915 Harley-Davidson

? Who raced on wooden boards?

Early motorcycle races used to take place on wooden bike tracks. Imagine the splinters if you fell off!

 Is it true?
All motorcycles have brakes.

NO. Motorcycles built for speedway racing have no brakes, and only one gear. These races take place on oval tracks made of dirt, sand, grass, and sometimes ice. The riders slide around the bends at each end of the track.

 Amazing! In high-speed crashes, motorcycle racers sometimes skid across the ground at 150 mph! So racers wear leather overalls to protect them in case they fall off. They also have tough knee pads sewn into their leathers because their knees touch the road as they lean into bends.

What is a superbike?

A superbike, such as this Ducati, is a very fast motorcycle, normally with an engine of 750 cc or bigger. The word "superbike" was first used to describe the Honda CB750 of the late 1960s. Superbikes are designed for high-speed racing but can also be used for touring on public highways.

Ducati superbike

Modified Triumph Thunderbird

Amazing! Chopper motorcycles and tricycle motorcycles are popular with motorcycle gangs such as the Hell's Angels. Hell's Angels wear all black—black leathers and black helmets.

What is a chopper?

A chopper is a customized bike with a low seat, high handlebars, and long front forks. The rider leans back, as if in an armchair. Choppers first appeared in the United States when Harley owners chopped up parts of bikes to make much lighter and faster versions.

Chopper

❓ Who reached 214 mph on a Triumph?

Johnny Allen rode a cigar-shape Triumph bike at 214 mph across the American Bonneville Salt Flats in 1956. Triumph named their most famous bike the Bonneville after this feat.

Is it true?

Chopped scooters are used for drag racing.

YES. A drag race is a race between two motorcycles along a short, straight track. Some drag racers compete on chopped scooters, which are scooters with a beefed up engine and a long frame.

❓ Who put three engines on a motorcycle?

Russ Collins put three engines onto his Honda drag racer in the 1970s. Drag bikes need a huge amount of power for maximum acceleration, and some models are even powered by rocket engines!

Russ Collins

Which racing bike has no front forks?

The Honda Elf Endurance racer was the first racing motorcycle without front forks. Instead of forks, the bike had lever arms to support the front wheel. It raced in the 1980s at Le Mans.

 Is it true?
Some motorcycles had steering wheels.

YES. The bizarre Militaire motorcycle of 1912 had a steering wheel instead of handlebars. Balancing was difficult, so the bike needed stabilizers.

Honda Elf

Which bike do you sit in?

The odd-looking BMW C1 is one of the few motorcycles that you sit inside. It has a seat like a car seat, but controls like a motorcycle. The open-sided hood protects the rider from the rain and wind.

BMW C1

Amazing! The smallest motorcycles are very tiny indeed! The world's smallest is 4 inches long, with wheels three quarters of an inch across. It has an engine and can be ridden (but only just!)

Which bike crossed the United States using less than 15 gallons of fuel?

The 1983 Heysercycle was covered in rounded bodywork to lessen air drag, and used only 1 gallon of fuel every 210 miles—a new record for fuel economy.

Heysercycle

? What is stunt riding?

Stunt riders speed up ramps on their bikes, and jump over cars, buses, and trucks. The most famous stunt rider of all, Evel Knievel, even tried to jump a canyon in a rocket-powered "skycycle" in 1974. He nearly drowned in the attempt. Evel claimed that he had broken every bone in his body! He died in 2007.

Evel Knievel

Amazing!

Teams of stunt riders perform incredible tricks, such as building motorcycle pyramids and jumping through rings of fire. For a pyramid, the team members balance on each other's shoulders while the bikes are moving.

Wall of death

? What is the wall of death?

The wall of death is a circular, vertical wall. Stunt riders whiz around and around it on their motorcycles, as if they're riding inside a can! They have to ride at full speed to avoid falling off the wall.

What is freestyle motocross?

Freestyle motocross is a new motorcycle sport where the riders perform daring tricks as they jump off humps on a dirt track. Sometimes they even let go of their bikes completely!

Is it true?
Riding on one wheel is impossible.

NO. Riders can lift their front wheels off the ground and ride along on the rear wheel. This trick is called a wheelie. Superbike racers do wheelies to celebrate winning a race.

Freestyle motocross

CHAPTER SIX

TRUCKS & DIGGERS

Which trucks had steam engines?

In the 19th century, the first powered trucks had steam engines, before gasoline engines and diesel engines were invented. They looked like the steam tractors used on farms.

Foden steam truck

 Amazing! The first ever steam-powered vehicle was destroyed in a crash. The three-wheeled carriage was built by French engineer Nicolas-Joseph Cugnot in 1769, and was supposed to pull artillery guns.

What did trucks look like before steam engines were invented?

Before steam engines were invented, cargo was moved in wagons pulled by animals, such as oxen or horses. This is why the first powered trucks and cars were called "horseless" carriages.

Wagon train

What was a charabanc?

A charabanc was a flat-bodied truck with benches in the back for passengers to sit on. The first charabancs were pulled by teams of horses in France, and the idea spread to Great Britain in the early 20th century.

Charabanc

Is it true?

Early buses were pulled by steam tractors.

YES. A steam tractor was a steam-powered vehicle designed for towing wagons. The first passenger-carrying buses were made up of a wagon with several seats inside, pulled by a steam tractor.

Cab-over truck

Is it true?
Diesel invented the diesel engine.

YES. The diesel engine, which is a type of internal combustion engine, was first demonstrated by German engineer Rudolph Diesel in 1897. Most trucks have diesel engines because they are usually more economical and more reliable than gasoline engines.

What is a cab-over truck?

A cab-over truck is a truck where the driver's cab is over the top of the engine. The whole cab tips forward so that a mechanic can reach the engine to repair it.

? What is the fifth wheel?

The fifth wheel is the swiveling connecting device on all articulated trucks, behind the cab on the tractor unit. Trailers link onto it. The fifth wheel lets the trailer swivel when the truck turns corners.

Fifth wheel

? What gives piggyback rides?

Truck tractor units are often delivered by being towed by another truck as though they were trailers. It saves money because the trucks being towed don't use up any fuel.

Kenworth piggyback trucks

How do truck drivers talk to each other?

Truck drivers talk to each other on citizens' band (CB) radios. They warn each other about traffic jams or bad weather. Drivers use nicknames, called handles, instead of their real names.

Trucker using CB radio

Amazing!
During the winter, some truck drivers build fires under their cabs while they are stopped! When diesel fuel gets very cold it goes thick and gooey, so drivers try to keep it warm and runny so that their engines will start again without any trouble.

Is it true?
Trucks have up to 16 gears.

YES. Trucks need a lot of gears. They need very low gears for starting off with a heavy load and for slowly climbing steep hills. They also need very high gears for traveling quickly on highways.

? Where do truckers sleep?

Some long-distance truck drivers sleep in bunks behind or over their seats. The biggest trucks have a sleeper compartment behind the cab, with a bathroom and shower.

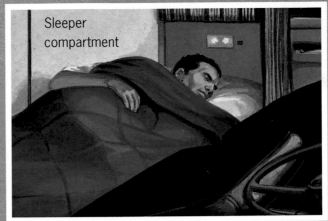

Sleeper compartment

Jackknifed truck

? What is a jackknife?

A jackknife happens when a truck driver tries to stop, but the trailer slides sideways, out of control. A jackknife is very dangerous—the trailer might turn over. It is named after a knife with a folding blade.

What is a monster truck?

A monster truck is an ordinary pickup truck fitted with huge dump-truck wheels, extra-strong suspension, and a very powerful engine. Monster truck owners race their trucks over tracks with huge bumps and jumps. The trucks bounce about and even tip over if they go too quickly.

Monster truck

 Is it true?
Monster trucks drive over cars.

YES. In monster truck racing, some of the obstacles that the trucks drive over are old cars! The cars get crushed flat under the trucks' massive wheels.

Bedford Afghan truck

Who paints trucks for protection?

In countries such as Afghanistan and India, truck drivers paint their trucks with bright colors and religious symbols. They believe that the symbols will stop them from having accidents.

Customized pickup truck

Amazing! Some of the most famous American monster trucks are called Grave Diggers. They have amazing custom paint jobs, with scenes of graveyards all over their bodywork!

What are customized trucks?

Customized trucks have special parts, such as huge wheels, high suspensions, and big engines. Some even have trunks, hoods, and doors moved by hydraulic rams. Custom trucks are built specially for shows and races.

169

❓ What is a dragster truck?

A dragster truck is customized for high-acceleration drag racing. Dragsters race against each other in pairs from a standing start along a short track. Dragsters have extra-powerful engines and enormous rear tires to get plenty of grip on the road.

Dragster trucks

Hawaiian Fire Department's jet truck

❓ What is the fastest truck?

The world's fastest truck is the Hawaiian Fire Department's custom-built fire truck. This truck was originally built in 1940, and is powered by two jet engines taken from aircraft! It can reach more than 400 miles per hour.

 ### Is it true?
You can race trucks.

YES. There's a lot of truck racing around the world. In the United States, drivers race customized pickup trucks. In Europe, they race big truck tractor units.

Leyland truck doing a wheelie

Can trucks do wheelies?

Customized pickup trucks can do wheelies. They have huge engines and a heavy weight at the rear to help the front rise up.

How do tanks travel?

Tanks are good at driving across rough, muddy ground, but they're very slow. When tanks need to move quickly, they're carried on special tank transporters. The transporter's trailer needs a lot of wheels to spread out the huge weight of the tank.

Oshkosh tank transporter

Amphibious trucks

Which trucks can swim?

Armies transport equipment in amphibious trucks that can drive on land like a normal truck and float across water like a boat. Amphibious trucks have a waterproof underside to stop water from flooding the engine.

 Amazing! Some trucks have armor plating on the outside. They're called armored personnel carriers (APCs for short). They're used to carry troops on battlefields.

What carries missiles?

Missile-carrying trucks transport huge nuclear missiles. Onboard the truck is a launchpad and a control center for launching the missile. The trucks carry the missiles into the countryside if their base is threatened by enemy attack.

Russian mobile missile launcher

Is it true?

Some trucks have caterpillar tracks.

YES. A type of truck called a half-track has wheels at the front and caterpillar tracks at the rear. Armies often transport their troops in half-tracks.

Which truck scrapes?

A scraper is a truck that scrapes a thin layer of soil from the ground and collects it. Scrapers move and level earth during road building.

Scraper

Excavator

What is a digger?

A digger is a machine that digs holes in the ground with a bucket on the end of an arm. The arm and bucket are moved by powerful hydraulic rams. Caterpillar tracks help the digger move across rough, muddy ground. Some diggers are called excavators.

Is it true?
Digger buckets can hold two cars.

YES. Huge diggers that work in quarries and opencast mines gouge rock and earth out with huge rotating bucket wheels. Each bucket could hold two cars.

174

Which are the biggest trucks in the world?

One of the world's biggest trucks was a dumper truck called a Terex Titan. It's as tall as a house and carried 300 tons of rubble. Even bigger is the Caterpillar 797B, which holds 380 tons.

Terex Titan

Amazing! Huge trucks, such as the Terex Titan, are too big to drive on public highways. So to get from one work site to another, they are taken apart and carried on transporter trucks.

175

? Which digger can do different jobs?

A type of digger called a backhoe loader can dig, load and drill. At the back is a digger arm with a bucket called a backhoe. At the front is a shovel for picking up loose soil and rock. Different sized buckets or a pneumatic drill can be attached to the backhoe.

 Is it true?
Some trucks have bullet-proof glass.

YES. Demolition machines have extra-strong, bulletproof glass in their cabs. The glass stops falling masonry from crashing into the cab and hurting the driver.

Backhoe loader

 **Amazing!** There are mini digging machines as well as big ones. Mini machines are used where large machines can't go, such as in basements, and for digging small trenches in pavements and yards.

Mobile crane

? Which trucks can reach high up?

A mobile crane is a truck with a crane on its back. Mobile cranes work on construction sites, lifting heavy objects, such as steel girders, into place with their telescopic arms. There is a cab at the back for the driver who operates the crane.

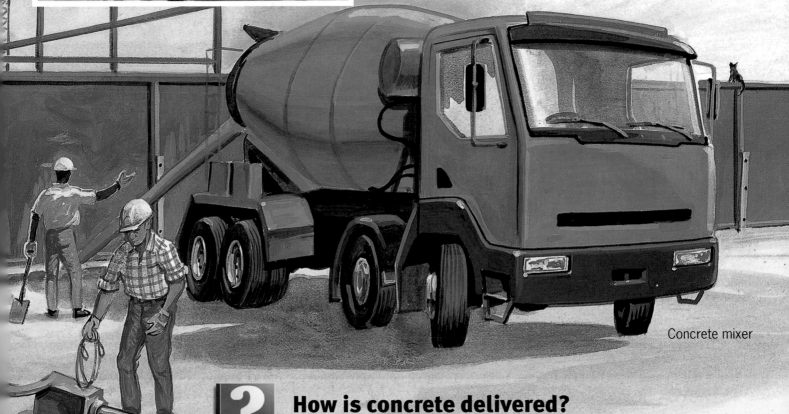
Concrete mixer

? How is concrete delivered?

Concrete is carried to construction sites in concrete mixers. The ingredients are put in the mixer's drum, which rotates, mixing the concrete.

? What are chains used for?

Strong metal chains called snow chains stop trucks from skidding on icy or snow-covered roads. The chains are wrapped around all the truck's tires and cut into the ice or snow, gripping it tightly. In cold countries, truck drivers always carry snow chains with them.

DAF Trucks
TURBO TWIN

Scania six-wheeler

Snow chains

Amazing! Some farm tractors have huge double sets of wheels to stop them from churning up the soil. In very muddy ground, normal tractors sink into the mud. Double wheels spread the tractor's weight over a bigger area to stop it from sinking.

DAF Turbotwin rally truck

❓ Which trucks race across the Sahara?

Trucks compete in many rallies, including the famous Dakar Rally that crosses the Sahara in northern Africa. More trucks carry spares and mechanics for other competitors, who race in cars and on motorcycles.

Four-wheel drive pickup truck

❓ What is four-wheel drive?

When a truck has four-wheel drive, it means that the engine makes all the wheels turn. In some trucks, the engine only turns two of the wheels. Four-wheel drive is good for driving off-road on muddy tracks.

? Can trucks move houses?

Very powerful trucks called tractors are used for pulling very heavy loads. They have monster diesel engines and can drive very slowly. Tractors can even move houses loaded onto wide trailers.

? Which truck carried a spacecraft?

In January 1977, the space shuttle Enterprise was transported 40 miles overland by a Kenworth diesel truck across the Mojave Desert in California. The shuttle weighed 75 tons, but the Kenworth was able to pull a load of over 500 tons.

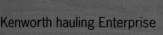
Kenworth hauling Enterprise

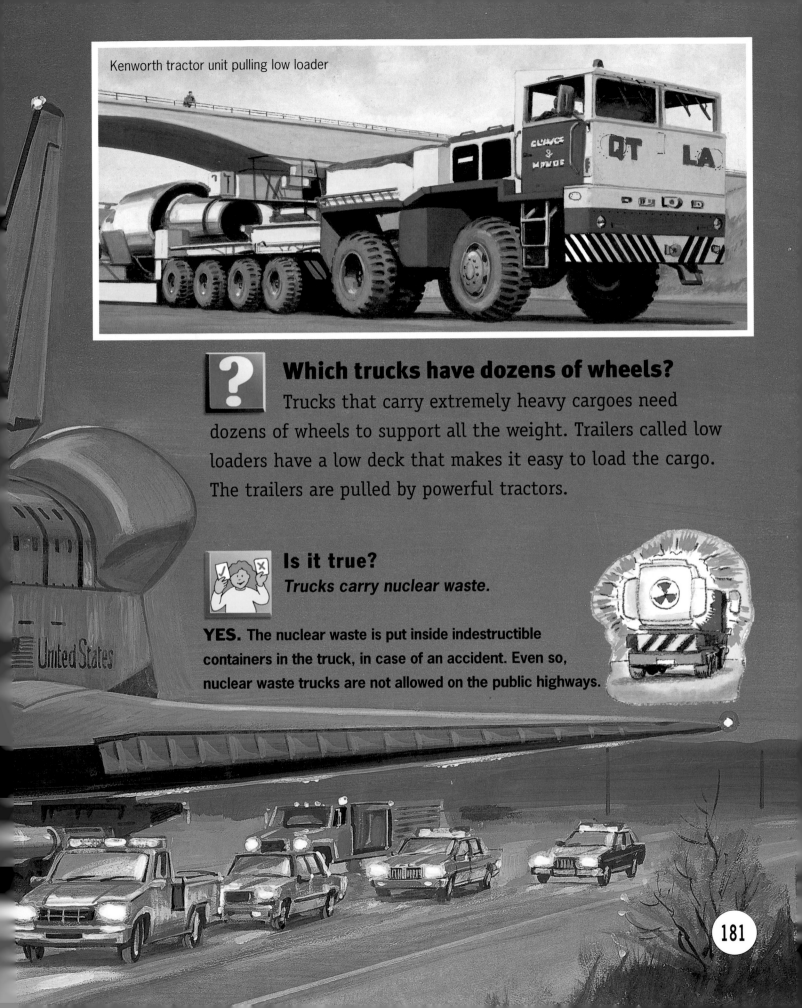

Kenworth tractor unit pulling low loader

? Which trucks have dozens of wheels?

Trucks that carry extremely heavy cargoes need dozens of wheels to support all the weight. Trailers called low loaders have a low deck that makes it easy to load the cargo. The trailers are pulled by powerful tractors.

Is it true?

Trucks carry nuclear waste.

YES. The nuclear waste is put inside indestructible containers in the truck, in case of an accident. Even so, nuclear waste trucks are not allowed on the public highways.

United States

 Amazing! Water is pumped along fire hoses by a powerful pump in a fire truck. It comes out of the hose nozzle so quickly that the firefighter holding the nozzle can be lifted off the ground.

? Which fire truck has two drivers?

Some fire trucks carry ladders so long that the ladder needs its own extra-long trailer. A second driver in a rear cab turns the rear wheels of the trailer so that the truck can get around sharp corners to reach fires in narrow streets.

Airport fire truck

 **Is it true?**
Fire trucks need stabilizers.

YES. Fire trucks with long ladders could topple over if the ladder was fully extended to the side. So they have two stabilizers on each side.

How far can a fire truck's ladder reach?

Some fire trucks have telescopic ladders, which are more than 130 feet long when fully extended. That's long enough to reach the 11th floor of a building.

Pierce Aerial Tiller fire truck

Who puts aircraft fires out?

Airports have their own teams of firefighters who use fleets of special fire trucks. The trucks fight fires with foam instead of water. The foam is fired from a cannon on top of the fire truck and smothers any fuel that is alight.

Amazing! Some cargo trucks carry a mini forklift truck with them for loading and unloading cargo. The forklift folds up and is carried attached to the back of the main truck.

? What is a wrecker?

A wrecker is a recovery truck that tows away cars, buses, and other vehicles that are wrecked in accidents, often blocking roads or lying in ditches. Wreckers need powerful diesel engines for towing and a winch for pulling vehicles that have tipped over back onto their wheels.

Wrecker

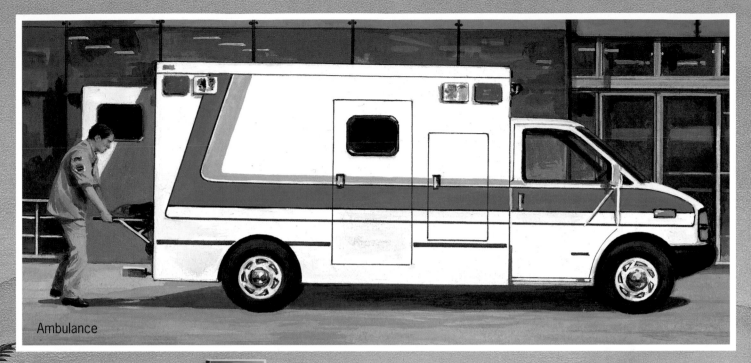

Ambulance

? Which truck saves lives?

An ambulance is a small truck specially adapted to carry injured and sick people quickly to hospital. There are stretchers for patients and emergency medical equipment in the back of the ambulance.

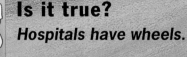

Is it true?

Hospitals have wheels.

YES. Mobile hospitals are mini hospitals inside a converted truck. They work in remote areas where people cannot get hospital treatment, and carry doctors, nurses, and even an operating room.

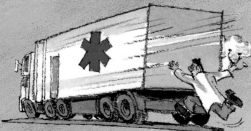

How do loggers load logs?

Log-carrying trucks have a small crane on the back with a strong grab on the end. The driver controls the grab, which lifts whole tree trunks stripped of their branches onto the truck. Bars on the trailer stop the logs from rolling off.

Logger

Amazing! Big car transporters can carry up to a dozen cars at once. They have cleverly designed decks and ramps, which allow the cars to drive on and off, and fold up so the cars fit into a tiny space.

Is it true?
Tankers carry chocolate.

NO. But tanker trucks can carry almost anything liquid, including milk and oil, and solids, such as flour.

What is a road train?

A truck with two or more trailers is called a road train because it looks like a train traveling on the road. Road trains have powerful tractor units and a big sleeper cab. They are used mainly in Australia.

Straddle truck

❓ What is a straddle truck?

A straddle truck is a type of mobile crane. It rolls over the load it is going to lift, with wheels on each side of the load. Straddle trucks often work in ports, lifting and moving cargo containers.

ROAD TRAIN

Australian road train

What needs a ramp to unload?

Dump trucks have a lifting body that tips up to make a load slide out. Sometimes whole trucks are tipped up by a ramp instead! This truck is unloading grain into a grain store.

Grain truck unloading

Garbage truck

188

Which truck tows aircraft?

Airport tugs pull aircraft around when the aircraft cannot use their engines. The tug has a tow bar that attaches to an aircraft's front wheel. Its low body doesn't bump into the fuselage.

Airliner tug

Is it true?

Cherry pickers are used to pick fruit.

NO. Cherry picker is the nickname for a truck with a working platform on the end of an extending arm. A worker on the platform can do jobs such as changing bulbs in streetlights.

Which trucks carry trash?

Garbage trucks drive around collecting trash. A mechanism lifts garbage cans, turns them upside down, and shakes them to empty their contents into the truck. Then a powerful ram crushes the trash and squeezes it into the truck.

189

CHAPTER SEVEN

AIRCRAFT

? Who were the first people to fly?

The first people to make a real flight were two Frenchmen, François Pilâtre de Rozier and the Marquis d'Arlandes. On November 21, 1783, they flew for 25 minutes over Paris in a hot-air balloon made by the Montgolfier brothers.

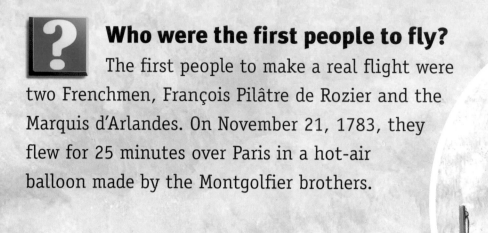

Montgolfier balloon

? Who built a steam plane?

The first airplane to leave the ground was the steam-powered Éole. It was built by French aviator Clément Ader, and had batlike wings. It only flew for about 55 yards in 1890, and could not be steered!

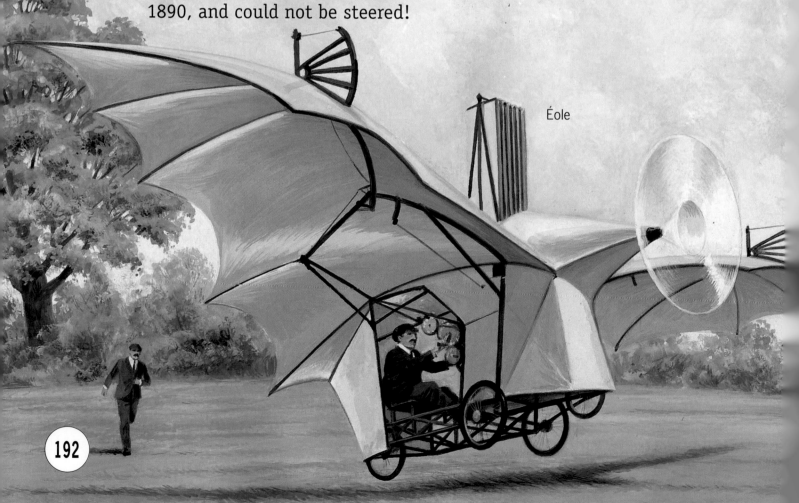

Éole

Who flew the first gliders?

The first person to build and fly gliders was the German engineer Otto Lilienthal. He made hundreds of flights, starting in 1891. Lilienthal launched himself from hills, and hung under his gliders. He was killed in a glider crash in 1896.

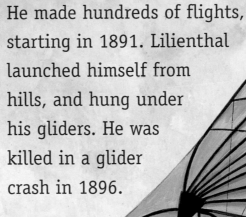

Otto Lilienthal

Amazing! In the 14th-century Chinese merchants launched kites with people tied to them to see if it was windy enough to set sail in their ships. If the kite failed to fly, they stayed in port until another day. This fact was reported by the famous European traveler Marco Polo.

Is it true?
People flew by flapping their arms.

NO. For hundreds of years people attempted to fly by strapping wings to their arms and flapping them. They became known as "birdmen," and many were injured or killed after they launched themselves from high buildings or cliffs. For humans, flying like birds is impossible because we do not have shoulder muscles that are strong enough for flapping.

❓ Who made the first airplane flight?

The first person to make a controlled flight in an airplane with an engine was Orville Wright. His flight took place in the airplane Flyer on December 17, 1903, at Kitty Hawk, North Carolina. The flight lasted just 12 seconds and was 40 yards long. Flyer was a biplane built by Orville and his brother Wilbur, who were bicycle makers.

Antoinette monoplane

Flyer

 Amazing! In 1914, the fastest aircraft were slower than the fastest racing cars. The world speed record for aircraft was just over 126 mph, but the world land-speed record was 140 mph. By 1920, aircraft had overtaken.

What is a monoplane?

A monoplane is an airplane with one pair of wings. Most early airplanes were biplanes, with two sets of wings. The graceful Antoinette VII of 1908 was one of the first monoplanes to fly.

Is it true?

One plane had 20 wings.

YES. In 1904, Englishman Horatio Phillips built a plane with 20 small wings, one above the other. It was a complete failure. In 1907, he built a plane with no less than 200 wings!

Blériot XI

Who was the first to fly across the English Channel?

The first cross-channel flight was made by Frenchman Louis Blériot in 1909. He made the trip in one of his own airplanes, a Blériot number XI monoplane. It took just 37 minutes to fly from France to England. Blériot won a generous cash prize.

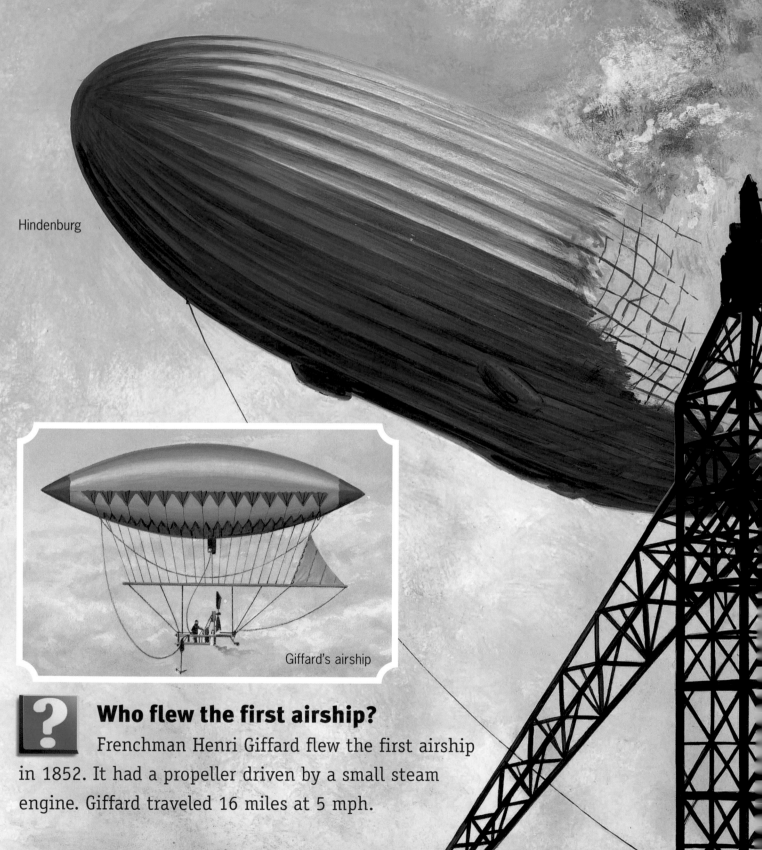

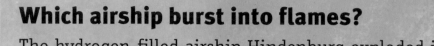 Which airship burst into flames?

The hydrogen-filled airship Hindenburg exploded in 1937, killing 35 of the 97 people onboard. It was one of the two largest airships ever. It was 268 yards long. That's two and a half soccer pitches!

Hindenburg

Giffard's airship

? Who flew the first airship?

Frenchman Henri Giffard flew the first airship in 1852. It had a propeller driven by a small steam engine. Giffard traveled 16 miles at 5 mph.

Amazing!

In 1802, Frenchman André Jacques Garnerin jumped from the basket of his hot-air balloon above London. He floated safely down under a parachute. It was the first successful parachute jump.

Breitling Orbiter

Is it true?

The first nonstop around-the-world balloon flight was in 1999.

YES. Bertrand Piccard and Brian Jones flew the Breitling Orbiter 3 from Chateaux D'Oex in Switzerland, and crossed the finishing line in Mauritania 19 days, 21 hours, and 55 minutes later. Piccard and Jones finally landed in the Egyptian desert.

Are airships used today?

Today, small airships fly above major sporting events. They carry television cameras to give viewers a bird's eye view of the action. They often have huge advertizing displays on their sides.

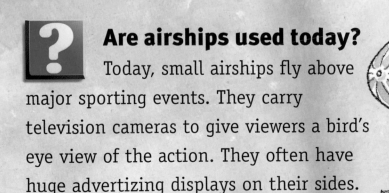

Who was the Red Baron?

The greatest fighter ace of World War I, Baron Manfred von Richthofen was known as the Red Baron. Between 1916 and 1918 he shot down 80 allied aircraft. He got his nickname from the bright red Fokker Dr I triplane he often flew in combat.

The Red Baron's Fokker Dr I triplane

Amazing! Some fighter pilots were not allowed to wear parachutes! During World War I, the commanders of the British Royal Flying Corps banned pilots, gunners, and navigators from carrying parachutes to escape from crippled aircraft.

Vickers Vimy

Is it true?
Pilots shot at their own propellers.

YES. During World War I, pilots fired machine guns at their own propellers. To start with, propellers were protected by metal plates. In 1915, a system was invented that made sure that the gun fired only when a propeller blade was not in the way.

Curtiss JN-4 "Jenny"

What were barnstormers?

Barnstormers were stunt pilots. They toured the United States in the 1920s, performing daredevil flying stunts, such as hanging from biplanes by their teeth. They also gave rides to the public. Barnstormers got their name by flying very low over farm buildings.

Who were the first people to fly across the Atlantic?

The first people to fly nonstop across the Atlantic were Britons Captain John Alcock and Lieutenant Arthur Whitten Brown. They flew in a twin-engined Vickers Vimy bomber, in 1919. It took more than 16 hours and ended with a crash into a bog!

199

Ryan M2 monoplane Spirit of St. Louis

? Who made the first solo flight across the Atlantic?

American pilot Charles Lindbergh made the first nonstop transatlantic solo flight in 1927. His all-metal Ryan monoplane, called Spirit of St. Louis, was built specially for the job. The flight took 33 hours and 30 minutes. Lindbergh tried to stay awake all the time to avoid crashing into the sea.

Amazing! U.S. Navy airman Richard E. Byrd was the first man to fly over both the North Pole and the South Pole. He reached the North Pole in May 1926 as navigator in a Fokker F VIIA and the South Pole in November 1929 as commander of a Ford tri-motor.

? Who was the first to fly across the Pacific?

In 1928, Australians Charles Kingsford Smith, Charles Ulm, and their navigators, made the first flight from the United States to Australia in a Fokker tri-motor. They refueled four times on Pacific islands.

Fokker tri-motor

Is it true?
The first solo airplane flight around the world took nearly eight days.

YES. The first around-the-world solo flight was made between July 15 and 22, 1933. Total flying time was 7 days, 18 hours, and 49 minutes for the 15,560 miles. The pilot was an American called Wiley Post, and his aircraft was a Lockheed Vega.

? Which woman flew solo from England to Australia?

English pilot Amy Johnson made the first solo England–Australia flight by a woman, in a Gypsy Moth biplane in 1930. She had many near disasters on the way, including almost flying into a mountain side.

Gypsy Moth

Amy Johnson

Surface-effect vehicle

YES. Experimental seaplanes called surface-effect vehicles fly very close to the water surface. Air squashed between their wings and the water helps to keep the plane flying. It means that the wings can be smaller than those on normal airplanes of the same size.

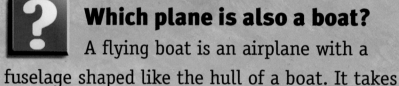

Which plane is also a boat?

A flying boat is an airplane with a fuselage shaped like the hull of a boat. It takes off and lands on water instead of a runway. During the 1930s, huge flying boats, such as the Short C-class Empire, were popular for traveling long distances.

Amazing! In 1938, a seaplane was carried into the air by a flying boat. The seaplane did not use any fuel to take off and so was able to fly nonstop across the Atlantic.

G-ADHK

Supermarine S 6B

In 1931, a Supermarine seaplane set a new world speed record, and won the Schneider Trophy. It was powered by a special Rolls–Royce engine and reached 406 mph!

? How do planes land on snow?

Airplanes can land on a flat stretch of snow or ice if they change their wheeled undercarriage for skis. One of the first planes with skis was a Fokker F VIIA used to fly over the North Pole. Modern ski planes take supplies to polar bases.

Short Maia flying boat

? Which planes have a hook?

Planes that land on aircraft carriers have a hook that drops down from the tail on landing. The hook drags along the runway, catches wires stretched across the deck, and the plane stops with a jolt.

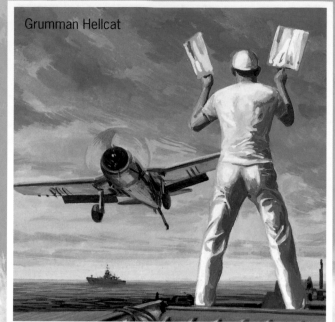
Grumman Hellcat

? What was a Flying Fortress?

The Boeing B-17 Flying Fortress was a four-engined heavy bomber flown by the Allies during World War II. It had thick armor and four swiveling gun turrets. In all, 12,731 Flying Fortresses were built between 1935 and 1945.

Flying Fortress

Who attacked out of the Sun?

World War II Japanese fighter pilots deliberately flew toward their targets from the direction of the Sun. This made it very difficult for enemy pilots and gunners to see the fighters because of the Sun's bright glare in the background.

P-51 Mustang

Amazing! The Northrop P-61 Black Widow hunted enemy planes at night. It was able to do this because it had a radar system in its nose. It was also painted black, making it very difficult to see in the night sky.

Is it true?
Some planes were made from wood.

YES. One World War II bomber, the de Havilland Mosquito, had a wooden frame and plywood on the wing and fuselage. This made the Mosquito very light, cheap to build, and very fast!

Who invented the jet engine?

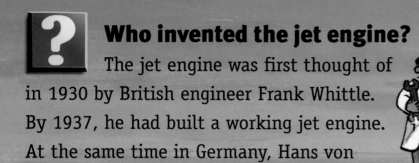

The jet engine was first thought of in 1930 by British engineer Frank Whittle. By 1937, he had built a working jet engine. At the same time in Germany, Hans von Ohain was building a similar engine.

de Havilland Comet

S·ALVO

BOAC

Heinkel He 178

Amazing! When the first jet-powered airplane took off on its maiden flight, it sucked a bird into its engine. The plane was the Heinkel He 178. All modern jet engines are designed to withstand "bird strikes," which could snap off the engine's fan blades and cause a crash.

❓ What was the first jet plane?

The first two jet planes were experimental fighters built during World War II. The German Heinkel He 178 flew in 1939 and the British Gloster E 28/39 in 1941.

Gloster E28/39

❓ What was the first jet airliner?

The first jet airliner to carry passengers was the de Havilland Comet I. It had four jet engines set into the wing roots. The first airline service using the Comet was begun in 1952 by the British Overseas Airways Corporation, between London and Johannesburg.

✔✘ Is it true?
Jet engines have fans.

YES. At the front of a jet engine there is an enormous fan that sucks in air. Large airliners have jet engines called turbofans, with fans as tall as a person. The fan compresses the air and forces it into the engine. Fuel burns in the air, creating a rush of hot gases, which blast out of the engine. They spin a turbine that works the fan.

Air pulled in and compressed by front fans

Compressed air and fuel burned in combustion chamber

Exhaust provides thrust

Is it true?
The first jet-to-jet combat took place during World War II.

NO. Jet fighters started flying on both sides near the end of World War II, but they never met in combat. The first time one jet fighter fought another was in 1950, during the Korean War. A USAF Lockheed F-80C shot down a Chinese MiG-15.

? Which fighter can swing its wings?

The Panavia Tornado has "swing" wings that can pivot backward and forward. The forward position is for takeoff and landing, because it gives plenty of lift when the airplane is moving slowly. After takeoff, the wings are swept back for high-speed flight.

Panavia Tornado

Amazing!
Fighter aircraft often fill up their fuel tanks while they are in the air. This is called in-flight refueling. The fuel comes from a large tanker aircraft. The fighter and tanker pilots have to fly very skillfully to connect up with the fuel hose dangling behind the tanker.

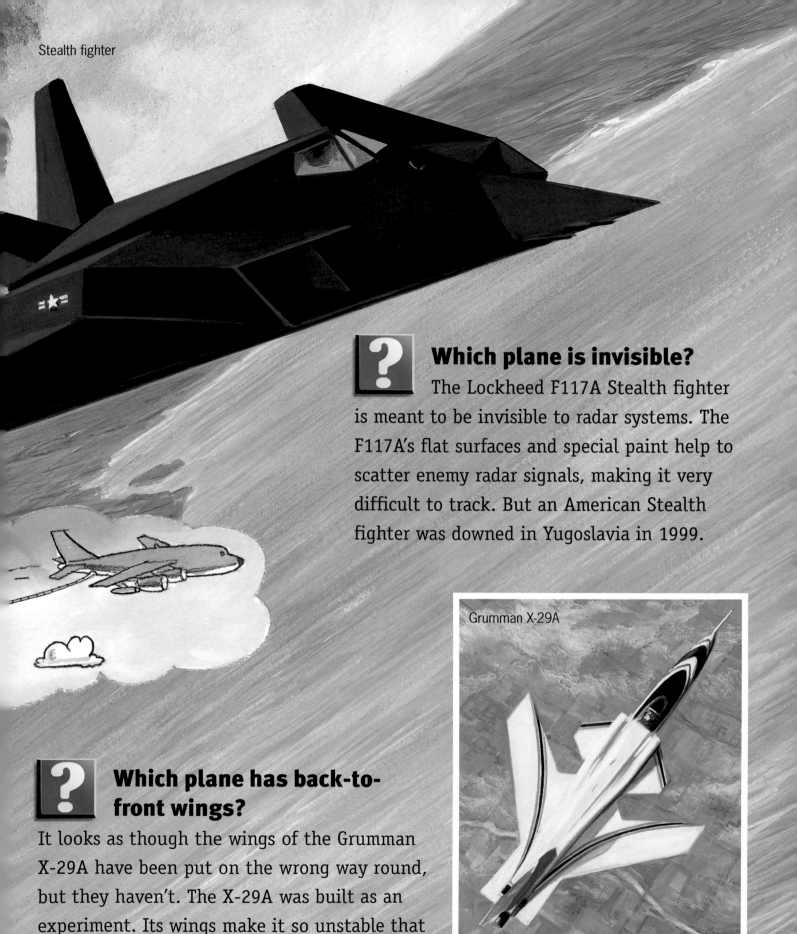

Stealth fighter

Which plane is invisible?

The Lockheed F117A Stealth fighter is meant to be invisible to radar systems. The F117A's flat surfaces and special paint help to scatter enemy radar signals, making it very difficult to track. But an American Stealth fighter was downed in Yugoslavia in 1999.

Grumman X-29A

Which plane has back-to-front wings?

It looks as though the wings of the Grumman X-29A have been put on the wrong way round, but they haven't. The X-29A was built as an experiment. Its wings make it so unstable that it can only be flown by computers.

❓ Which airliners carry the most people?

Seats for up to 660 passengers can be fitted into the most modern model of the two-deck Boeing 747 "Jumbo Jet"— the 747-400. The Airbus A380, which first flew in 2005, can carry more than 800 people in economy class.

Amazing! One gigantic flying boat with eight engines, the Hughes H4 Hercules, measured nearly 110 yards from one wing tip to the other and could have carried 700 passengers! Nicknamed "Spruce Goose," it only flew once in 1947 and is now in a museum.

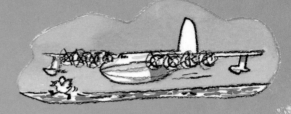

Boeing 747 "Jumbo Jet"

Antonov An-225

❓ Which is the biggest plane?

The biggest plane in the world is the six-engined Antonov An-225 transport airplane. It can carry other aircraft on its back as well as cargo inside. It can take off weighing a massive 640 tons.

YES. Monster military transport planes, such as the Lockheed C5 Galaxy and Antonov An-124, are big enough for tanks. The Galaxy can lift two 50-ton tanks, which drive in up ramps in the nose or tail.

Which transatlantic airliners have only two engines?

The Boeing 777 was the first airliner to fly across the Atlantic on a regular service with only two engines. Before 1984, all transatlantic airliners had three or four engines in case one failed. Now, engines are more reliable.

? Which plane traveled at 4,500 mph?

On October 3, 1967, an American X-15 rocket-powered airplane reached 4,500 mph. It's still the world record speed for an airplane. The X-15 also holds the altitude record of 354,200 feet. That's nearly 67 miles above Earth's surface!

X-15 rocket plane

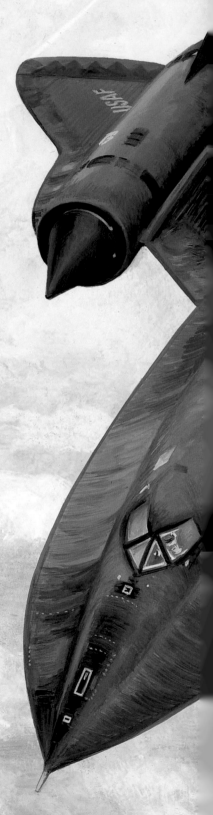

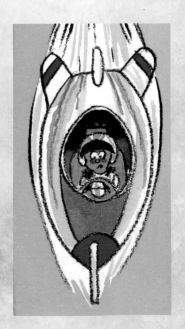

? Which plane had no wings?

In the 1970s, U.S. Air Force pilots flew an experimental plane called the X-24A without wings. This rocket plane had a specially shaped fuselage, or lifting body, to keep airborne.

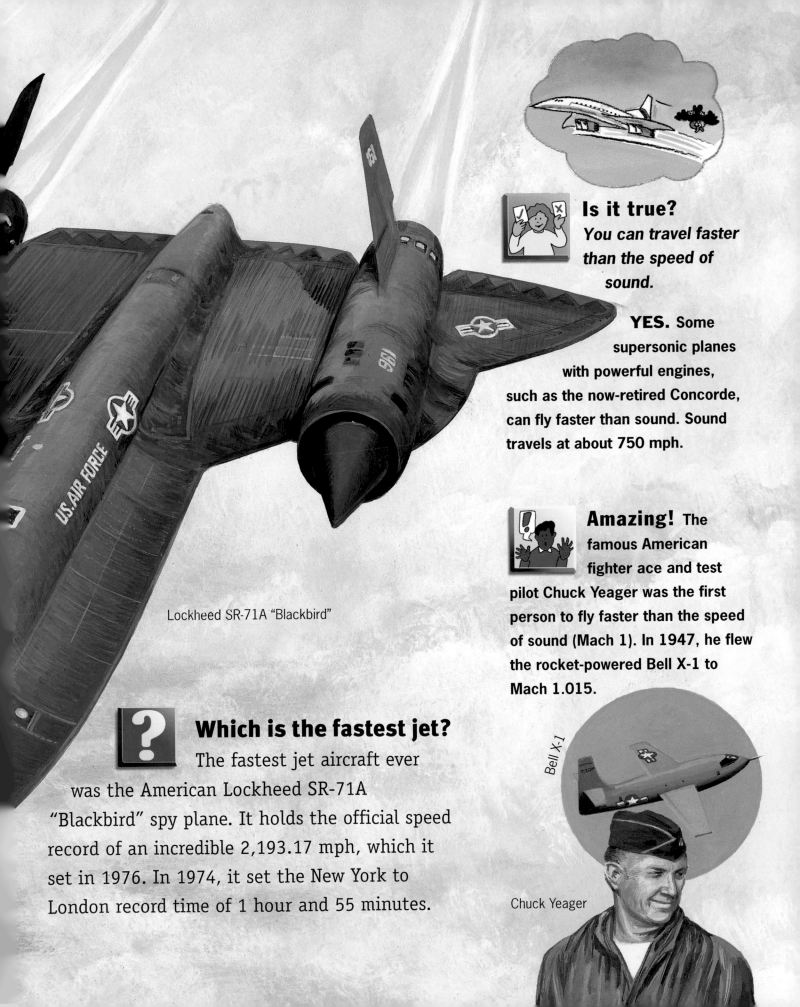

Lockheed SR-71A "Blackbird"

Is it true?
You can travel faster than the speed of sound.

YES. Some supersonic planes with powerful engines, such as the now-retired Concorde, can fly faster than sound. Sound travels at about 750 mph.

Amazing! The famous American fighter ace and test pilot Chuck Yeager was the first person to fly faster than the speed of sound (Mach 1). In 1947, he flew the rocket-powered Bell X-1 to Mach 1.015.

Bell X-1

Chuck Yeager

Which is the fastest jet?
The fastest jet aircraft ever was the American Lockheed SR-71A "Blackbird" spy plane. It holds the official speed record of an incredible 2,193.17 mph, which it set in 1976. In 1974, it set the New York to London record time of 1 hour and 55 minutes.

Which jet plane can hover?

The Harrier attack aircraft can take off and land vertically and also hover in the air. The exhaust from its jet engines comes out of four swiveling nozzles. For hovering, the nozzles point downward. For forward flight, they point backward.

Amazing!

Engineers built a bizarre machine nicknamed the "Flying Bedstead" to test vertical takeoff and landing aircraft. It had two jet engines, and its real name was the Thrust Measuring Rig.

de Havilland Dash 7

Which planes can take off and land in cities?

Aircraft such as the Dash 7 and 8 fly between small airports with short runways that are often near city centers. The Dash can take off and land on a runway only a few hundred yards long.

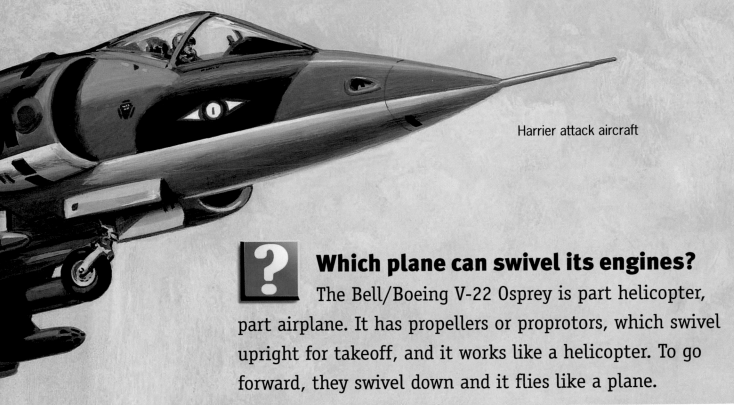
Harrier attack aircraft

❓ Which plane can swivel its engines?

The Bell/Boeing V-22 Osprey is part helicopter, part airplane. It has propellers or proprotors, which swivel upright for takeoff, and it works like a helicopter. To go forward, they swivel down and it flies like a plane.

Bell/Boeing V-22

✓✗ Is it true?
People can fly with jet packs.

YES. By strapping on the Bell rocket belt, a pilot could take off and hover in the air. At the beginning of the movie Thunderball, James Bond escapes from his enemies with one. However the amount of fuel stored in the rocket belt limits the flying time to less than 30 seconds.

❓ Why are helicopters used for rescuing people?

Helicopters make good rescue aircraft because they can hover in the air and land in small spaces. At sea, they hover while the crew pull people from the water. They are also used to lift injured mountaineers to hospital.

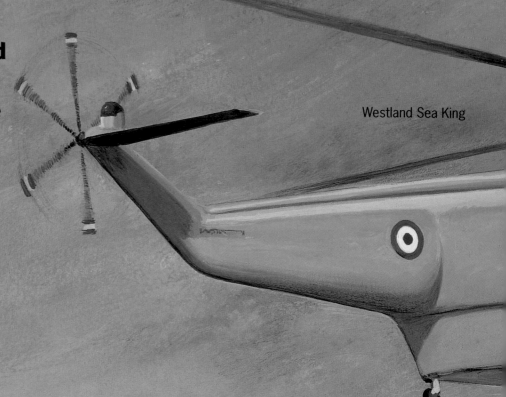

Westland Sea King

Sikorsky VS-300

❓ Who invented the first true helicopter?

People had been making brief helicopter flights since 1907, but the first successful helicopter flight was in 1939, when inventor Igor Sikorsky flew his VS-300. This had a single main rotor and a tail rotor, and was the ancestor of all modern helicopters.

 Amazing! Helicopters can be used as cranes! "Skycranes" can move heavy objects over short distances. They have a cargo space where the fuselage normally is.

216

Is it true?
All helicopters have two rotors.

NO. Very modern helicopters have a tail thruster instead of a second rotor, but most helicopters do have two rotors. As the engine spins the main rotor one way, it also tries to spin the fuselage the other way. A second rotor on the tail stops this from happening. On twin-rotor helicopters, the main rotors spin in opposite directions, so no tail rotor is needed.

Autogyro

? **What is an autogyro?**
An autogyro has a rotor that is not driven by an engine. As the autogyro is pushed along by its propeller, the rotor spins around automatically, providing the lift that keeps the autogyro in the air.

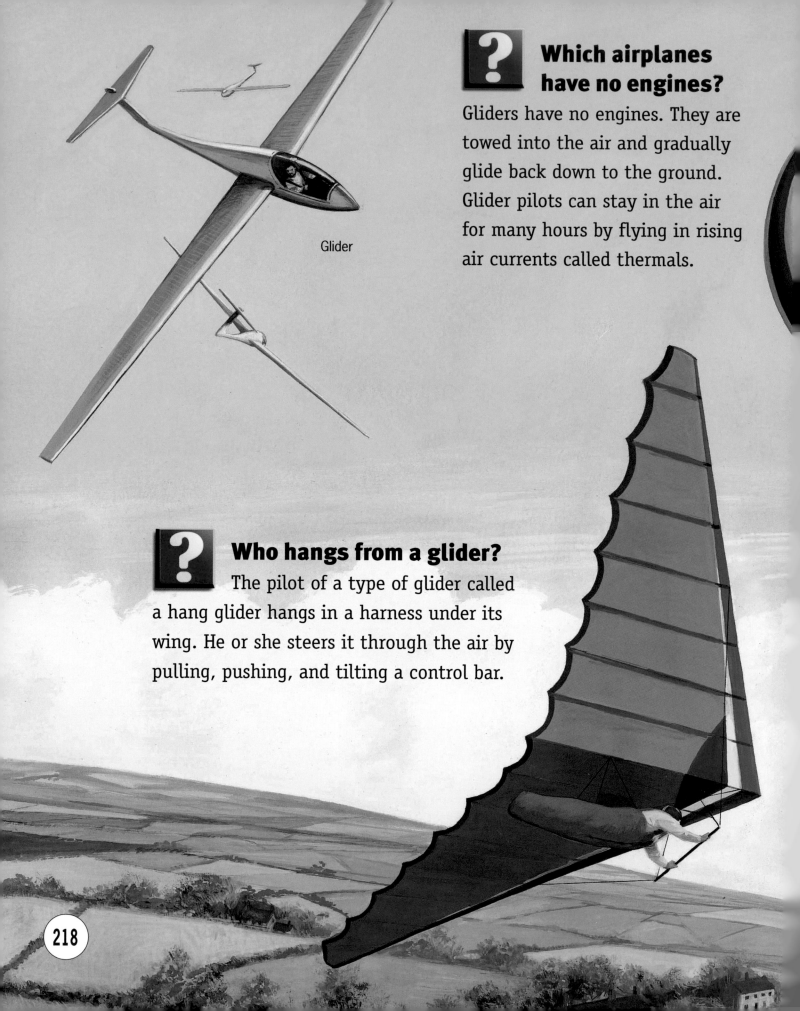

Glider

Which airplanes have no engines?

Gliders have no engines. They are towed into the air and gradually glide back down to the ground. Glider pilots can stay in the air for many hours by flying in rising air currents called thermals.

Who hangs from a glider?

The pilot of a type of glider called a hang glider hangs in a harness under its wing. He or she steers it through the air by pulling, pushing, and tilting a control bar.

Hot-air balloon

 Amazing! Pilots of paragliders can strap tiny engines to their backs to make a tiny plane. A paraglider is a little like a parachute that fills up with air to make a wing. The pilot hangs in a harness under the wing.

 Who flies on hot air?

Pilots and passengers in hot-air balloons are held up by hot air. A gas burner heats the air inside the balloon, making it hotter and lighter than the colder air outside. This makes the balloon float upward like an air-filled ball under water.

Is it true?
The space shuttle is a glider.

YES. The space shuttle is lifted up into space by huge rockets, but lands back on Earth as a glider. The two solid fuel boosters fall away as it takes off, so the pilot only has one chance to get the landing right.

CHAPTER EIGHT

SPACECRAFT

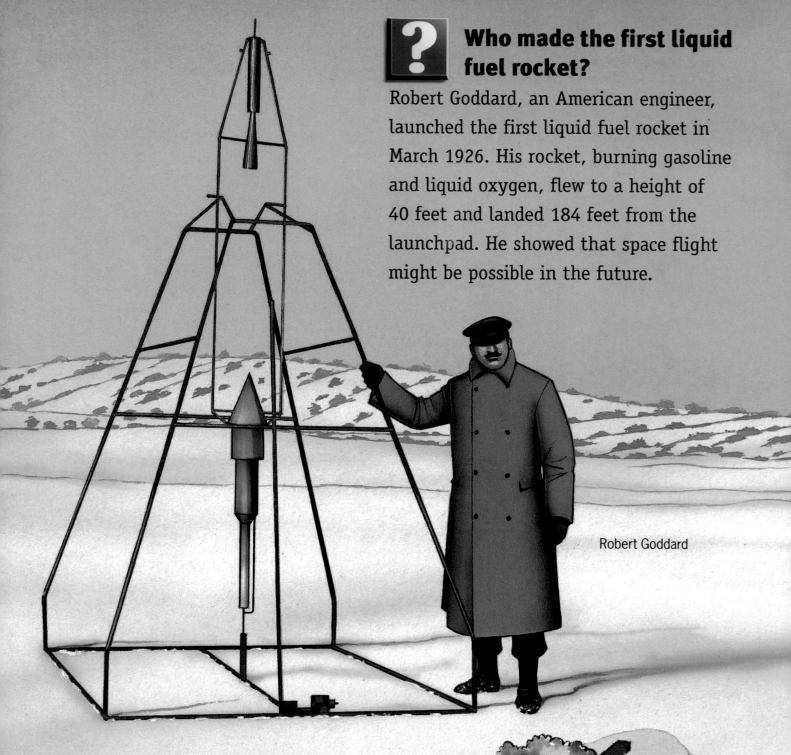

? Who made the first liquid fuel rocket?

Robert Goddard, an American engineer, launched the first liquid fuel rocket in March 1926. His rocket, burning gasoline and liquid oxygen, flew to a height of 40 feet and landed 184 feet from the launchpad. He showed that space flight might be possible in the future.

Robert Goddard

 Amazing! The Chinese invented rockets around the beginning of the last millennium! Powered by an early version of gunpowder, Chinese rockets in A.D. 1000 looked like fireworks. They were used in battle as flaming arrows! For the last 1,000 years, most big advances in rocket design have been made as a result of war.

What did the first satellite do?

Sputnik 1 was launched into orbit by Soviet Russia on October 4, 1957, 121 days ahead of its American rival, Explorer 1. Sputnik 1 circled the Earth once every 90 minutes, sending radio messages for 21 days, which the world listened to on the radio.

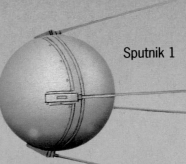

Sputnik 1

German V2 rocket

Is it true?
Rockets were used in World War II.

YES. The German scientist Wernher von Braun made rockets that could launch bombs across the English Channel. They damaged London without risking the lives of German pilots. Von Braun's V2 rocket was so successful, that after the war the United States gave him a job helping with its space program.

Who was the first earthling in space?

Before the first humans went to space, animals paved the way. Laika, a Russian mongrel dog, was the first earthling in space. Her seven days in orbit proved that space travel would be safe for humans.

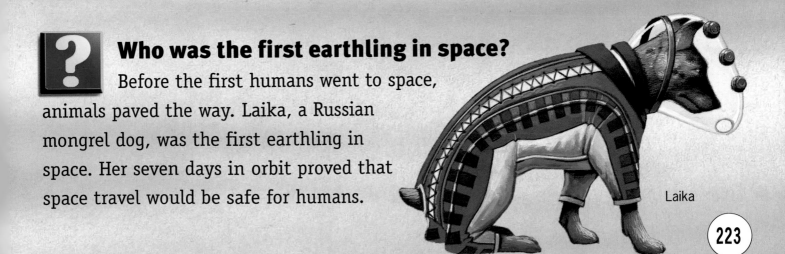

Laika

What was the biggest rocket ever?

American Saturn 5 rockets were 364-foot tall monsters, weighing 2,903 tons on the launchpad. That's as heavy as 600 elephants! They were more greedy than elephants, too, burning 15 tons of fuel per second. Saturn 5 rockets were used to launch all the Apollo missions to the Moon.

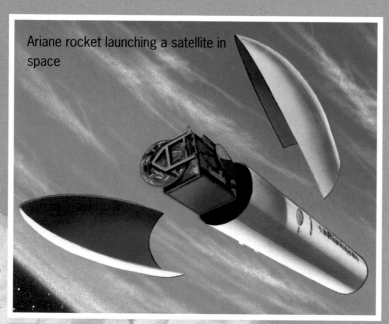

Ariane rocket launching a satellite in space

What do rockets carry?

Rocket cargo is called the payload, the load that pays for the trip. Most rockets are designed to carry one or two satellites. Some satellites are for scientific research, some are for communication, and some are for spying. Of course, rockets can also carry people!

Saturn 5

 Is it true?
Jet planes can fly in space.

NO. Jet engines need to take oxygen from the air around them to burn fuel. Because there's no air in space, a jet engine wouldn't work up there.

? **Why do rockets have stages?**

Rockets have to be big to carry enough fuel to escape Earth's pull. But once the fuel is burned, those big engines and fuel tanks are useless. Their weight would make visiting the Moon very difficult. So rockets are made in stages, or pieces, which drop off when they've done their job.

Saturn 5

 Amazing! Three German engineers made a rocket-powered car in 1928! Fritz von Opel, Max Valier, and Friedrich Sander tested the first version, Opel-Rak 1, on March 15, 1928. Opel later used the rocket knowledge he learned from Valier to fit 16 rockets onto a glider plane. It was the second ever rocket-powered aircraft.

Launch escape system

Command module

Service module

Lunar module inside

Stage 3 contains fuel and rocket engines

Stage 2 contains fuel and rocket engines

Stage 1 contains fuel and rocket engines

225

Who was the first person in space?

Yuri Gagarin, a 27-year-old Soviet pilot, orbited Earth on April 12, 1961. He spent 90 minutes in space in the Vostok 1 spacecraft before returning safely to Earth. Gagarin ejected from his capsule 3 miles above ground, landing by parachute near a very surprised six-year-old girl.

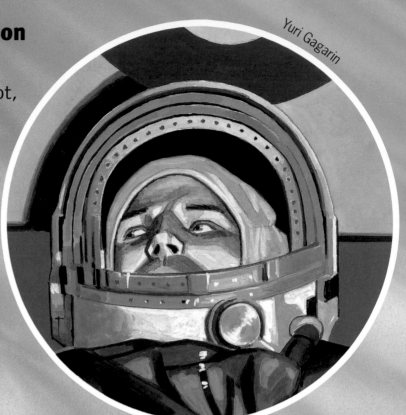

Yuri Gagarin

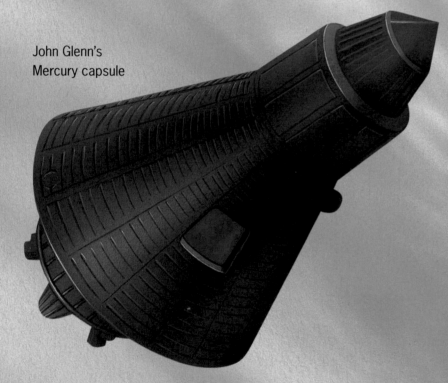

John Glenn's Mercury capsule

 ## Who was the first American in space?

Alan Shepard just reached space on May 5, 1961. He stayed only a few seconds, but he inspired the United States to reach for the Moon. John Glenn was the first American to orbit Earth.

Amazing! You can see the Great Wall of China from space. Especially at sunset and sunrise, the wall casts a very sharp shadow across the Chinese landscape and is visible to the naked eye. Without the help of a telescope, you can also make out city lights, and even supertankers!

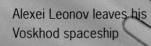

Alexei Leonov leaves his
Voskhod spaceship

? Who made the first space walk?

Alexei Leonov walked in space on March 18, 1965. He was roped to his space capsule to stop him from floating away. His space suit ballooned with air, and he had to let most of it out before he could fit back inside the capsule!

Is it true?
Sally Ride was the first woman in space.

NO. Valentina Tereshkova, a Soviet Russian textile worker, retrained as a pilot. She blasted into space on June 16, 1963, staying up in Vostok 6 for nearly three days. Later that year, she married another Soviet space traveler, Andrian Nikolayev. Sally Ride was the first American woman to reach space, on the space shuttle Challenger, in 1983.

Valentina Tereshkova

227

Neil Armstrong

? Who was the first person on the Moon?

Neil Armstrong was the first man to step onto the surface of the Moon, on Sunday, July 20, 1969. Armstrong called it one small step for a man, one giant leap for mankind. He was followed out by Buzz Aldrin, while Michael Collins orbited the Moon above them.

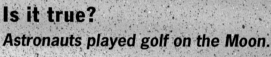

Is it true?
Astronauts played golf on the Moon.

YES. Apollo 14 arrived on the Moon in February, 1971, flown by Alan Shepard, America's first man in space, and Edgar Mitchell. They took rock samples and did some scientific experiments. After completing all their serious research work, Alan Shepard took out a golf club he had put together, and struck a few balls. They flew 400 yards in the low Moon gravity, much farther than they would have done on Earth.

Amazing! There is no wind on the Moon, so flags need a wire along the top to hold them out straight. The first flag was planted by Armstrong and Aldrin. They put it so close to their lander that it was knocked over when they blasted off.

Who took a car to the Moon?

The Apollo 15 crew took a Lunar Rover to the Moon in 1971. David Scott and James Irwin drove the battery-powered car around at speeds up to 7 mph. It had a satellite dish, a TV camera, and baskets to carry moon rocks.

Lunar Rover

Apollo 13

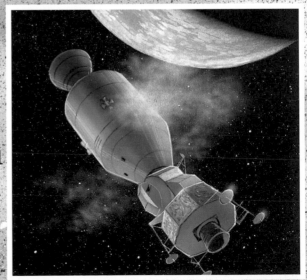

For whom was the number 13 unlucky?

James Lovell and his crew were flying to the Moon in Apollo 13, on April 13, 1970, when vital oxygen tanks exploded, disabling the spacecraft. The Moon mission was canceled. Ground Control worked very hard, and managed to bring them home successfully.

How do you fit into a space suit?

Space suits are almost as complicated as spacecraft. They must fit astronauts' bodies well, but they are made about 2 inches too tall on purpose! That's how much longer your spine becomes in weightlessness.

Is it true?
Astronauts get space sickness.

YES. Weightlessness can confuse your body's senses, making you vomit. Obviously, an astronaut's tummy must settle down before any space walking is allowed.

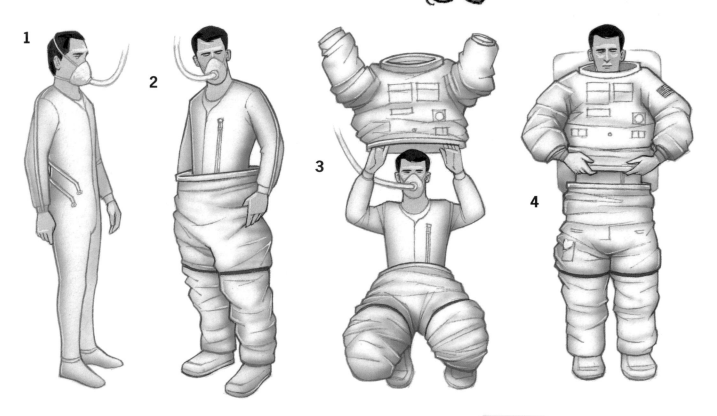

1 Get into special temperature-controlled underwear. **2** Slip on the lower body suit, with space boots, and plug in your diaper. **3** Slip into the top half from below. **4** Lock upper and lower parts together with metal connectors. **5** Put on the radio headset and check the microphone is working. **6** Lock gloves to the suit at the wrist with metal connectors. **7** Add your helmet and lock it into place. **8** Check that life support systems are working before climbing out through an airlock!

Amazing! Since you can't hold your nose in a space suit, it does it for you! There is a device inside the helmet that pinches your nose if you press against it. Astronauts can use this to hold their noses while they blow to pop their ears when the pressure changes.

Underwater training

Who trains in a water tank?

Working in a bulky space suit in orbit takes a lot of practice, but there's no room for mistakes in space. So astronauts practice in water tanks on Earth, which gives a feeling of weightlessness.

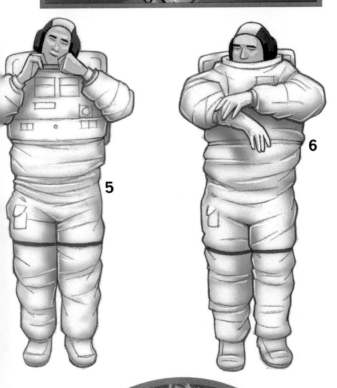

5

6

7

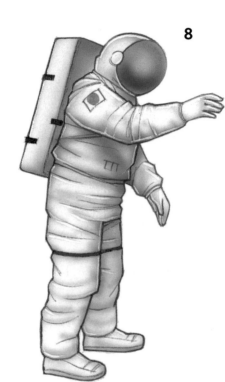

8

Why do astronauts need space suits?

Space is a vacuum (it has no air), so it's deadly for humans. Space suits give astronauts air to breathe, keep temperatures comfortable, and block radiation. They also stop your body from exploding!

Who returned to Earth at 38,600 mph?

If you rub your hands together very fast, they warm up. Imagine how hot capsules became as they rubbed against the atmosphere at 38,600 mph! Before the shuttle, all astronauts returned from space in capsules. A heat shield protected the crew from 6,360°F temperatures outside.

Capsule entering Earth's atmosphere

Is it true?

All spacecraft are reusable.

NO. Only the American space shuttles and the Russian Buran spaceplane are reusable. The shuttle uses rocket boosters to reach orbit, which drop off and parachute back to Earth, though the fuel tank can't be reused.

Who parachuted into the ocean?

Once the air slowed a capsule down, the astronauts inside released large parachutes. These acted as giant brakes, letting the capsule land softly on water. Once landed, the astronauts could be picked up by helicopter. All the Moon-walking astronauts splashed down at sea.

 ## Which space travelers had ejector seats?

Soviet Russia had no safe ocean to use, so cosmonauts had to land on solid ground. They used ejector seats to abandon their plummeting capsule about 3 miles above ground. Then they parachuted gently down to Earth.

 Amazing! Russia calls its space travelers cosmonauts, meaning "sailors of the universe." Americans think astronaut is a better word, meaning "sailor of the stars."

What do astronauts eat?

Astronauts take dehydrated (waterless) food into space, which weighs less than normal food. As their spacecraft burns hydrogen and oxygen in orbit, it creates water, which they add to their food. Astronauts eat slowly to stop food from flying around!

Mealtime in space

Astronauts testing space shuttle shower

Is it true?

Astronauts can't wash in space.

NO. The American Skylab space station (1973–74) had a shower. Astronauts climbed into a bag to wash, and water was vacuumed away. There are no showers on shuttles though. The crew use sanitary wipes.

Amazing! Shrimp, spiders, flies, bees, jellyfish, frogs, and goldfish have been to space! Animals were first used to test whether space travel would kill humans. The first creature to orbit the Moon was a tortoise!

How long can you stay in space?

Nobody knows! Weightlessness makes your heart lazier and your bones weaker. The biggest danger is radiation, but with exercise and shielding, you could stay in space for ages!

Shuttle docking with Mir space station

How do you go to the bathroom in space?

Very carefully! Once you're strapped to the toilet, it draws air into the bowl like a vacuum cleaner. Liquids are shot into space. Solids are taken home.

235

? Which spacecraft is reusable?

The space shuttle was the world's first reusable spacecraft. Instead of a stack of rocket stages, it has separate booster rockets and a big fuel tank. The shuttle drops these before reaching orbit. It eventually glides back to Earth using its wings.

3

3 Eventually the shuttle returns to Earth to be used again.

2 The fuel tank is jettisoned and burns up in the atmosphere. This is the only part that isn't reused.

2

1 The rocket boosters detach themselves and float back to Earth by parachute to be reused.

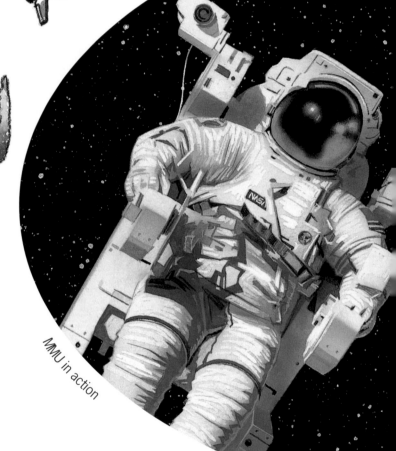

MMU in action

? What is an MMU?

The Manned Maneuvering Unit, or MMU, is a small strap-on spacecraft. Together with a space suit, the MMU lets an astronaut move freely through space. It uses 24 tiny jets of gas to travel in any direction.

Amazing! The shuttle has a special area for cargo. It can hold up to 29 tons. That's the size and weight of an adult humpback whale!

What does the space shuttle do?

The shuttle was first used for taking large satellites into orbit. After one shuttle blew up in 1986, NASA decided to use unmanned rockets again for launching satellites. The shuttles are now involved in research, repairing satellites in orbit, and building the International Space Station (ISS).

Shuttle nose tiles

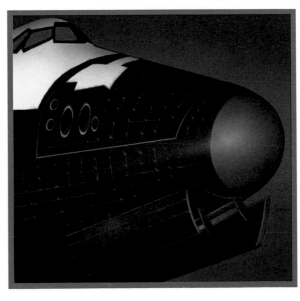

Is it true?
The shuttle is protected by tiles.

YES. The shuttle is made from aluminum. This metal is very light, but it melts at high temperatures. A shuttle can heat up to 6,360°F as it returns to Earth, so it needs 20,000 heat-proof tiles, which are glued onto its nose and belly.

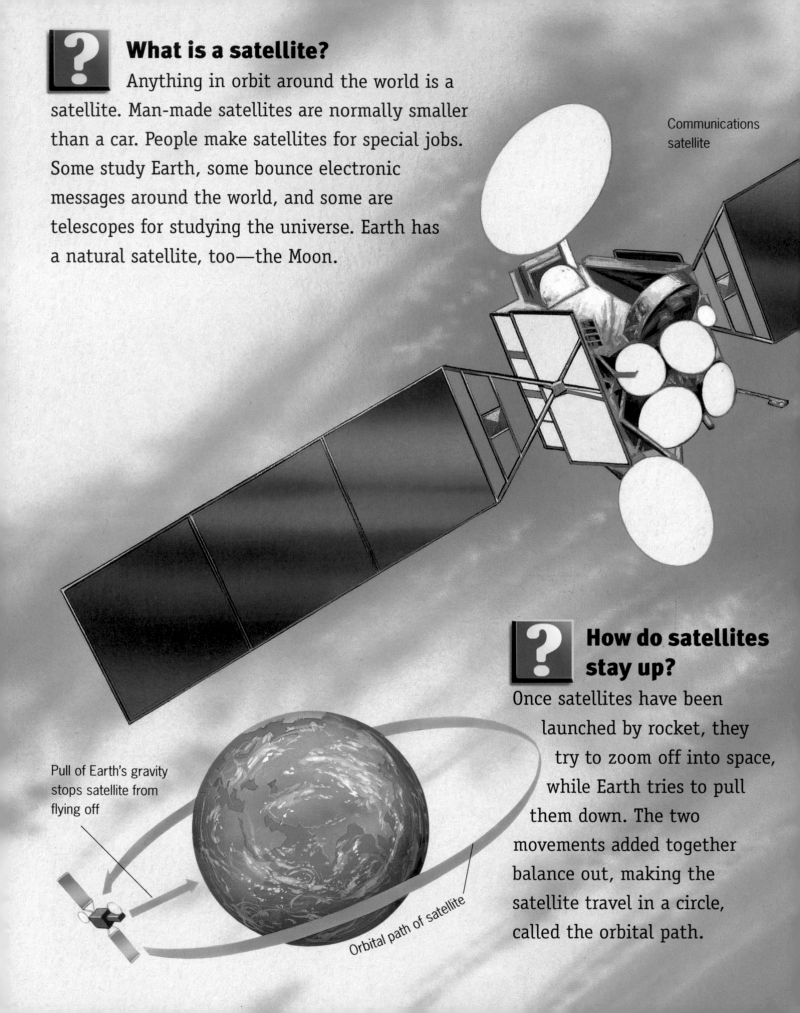

? What is a satellite?

Anything in orbit around the world is a satellite. Man-made satellites are normally smaller than a car. People make satellites for special jobs. Some study Earth, some bounce electronic messages around the world, and some are telescopes for studying the universe. Earth has a natural satellite, too—the Moon.

Communications satellite

? How do satellites stay up?

Once satellites have been launched by rocket, they try to zoom off into space, while Earth tries to pull them down. The two movements added together balance out, making the satellite travel in a circle, called the orbital path.

Pull of Earth's gravity stops satellite from flying off

Orbital path of satellite

Do satellites ever fall out of the sky?

Yes, accidents can happen! Satellites have crashed into the ocean, and pieces of the empty space station Skylab were found on farm land in Australia, after it fell back to Earth in 1979.

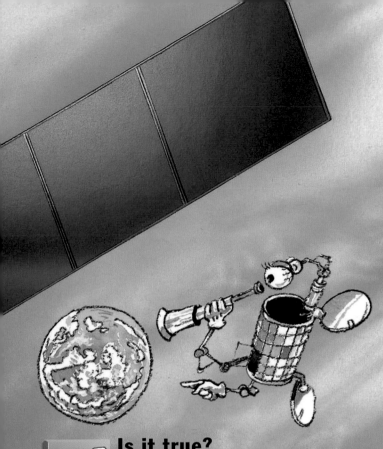

Is it true?

There are spy satellites in the sky.

YES. A big reason for the space race between Russia and the United States was to spy on each other. Spy satellites use telescopic cameras. Early spy satellites used to drop films to Earth by parachute. Now they take digital photos and beam them home, using secret codes.

Satellite crashing into the ocean

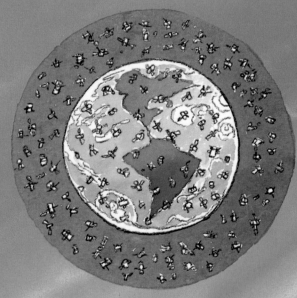

Amazing! There are 150,000 pieces of space garbage! They fly at incredible speeds, making them very dangerous. A window on a space shuttle was chipped once by a collision with a flake of paint! The American air force keeps track of the largest 8,500 objects in orbit. Letting garbage drop and burn up in the atmosphere helps to clean up space.

❓ Is there a telescope in space?

Astronomers on Earth have their view spoiled by our cloudy, dirty atmosphere, which makes stars seem to twinkle. There is no air in space, so distant objects are much clearer. The Hubble Space Telescope has taken photos of galaxies 13 billion light-years away!

Hubble telescope

Amazing! You can join space telescopes together to make one huge eye in the sky! First, a lot of small space telescopes have to be launched into space. Then they need to line up, like beads on a very big necklace. Computers compare what each telescope can see, and fill in the gaps. This can make a virtual telescope as big as a city!

Repairing Hubble

Is it true?

The Hubble telescope can see stars being born.

YES. The Hubble image here shows stars being made in the Eagle Nebula. The fingers of cloud are bigger than our entire solar system. They are made of gas and dust, which slowly collects into lumps. As they grow, the lumps become hotter, creating thousands of new stars!

Eagle Nebula

What happens if the telescope breaks down?

Hubble had to be fixed by astronauts almost as soon as it was launched. The mirror it uses to collect images was the wrong shape, making pictures fuzzy. In December 1993, a shuttle met up with Hubble, and astronauts adjusted the mirror successfully.

241

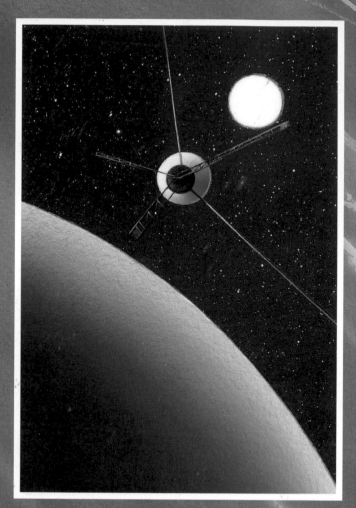

Voyager probe passing Neptune

Which voyagers visited all the planets?

Humans can't travel to other planets yet. A trip to Mars would need much bigger spacecraft than the shuttle. Instead, unmanned space probes such as Voyager can travel through the solar system, sending home pictures of the planets.

Is it true?
A *Mariner* took photos of Mercury.

YES. A very successful space probe called Mariner 10 visited the planet Mercury three times in the 1970s. As well as taking photos, Mariner discovered Mercury's strange magnetic field, and signs of ice at the poles.

Venera probe

Which probe got too hot?

Four Venera probes have landed on Venus. The temperature there is a sweaty 1,020°F. As if that wasn't bad enough, the clouds rain pure sulfuric acid!

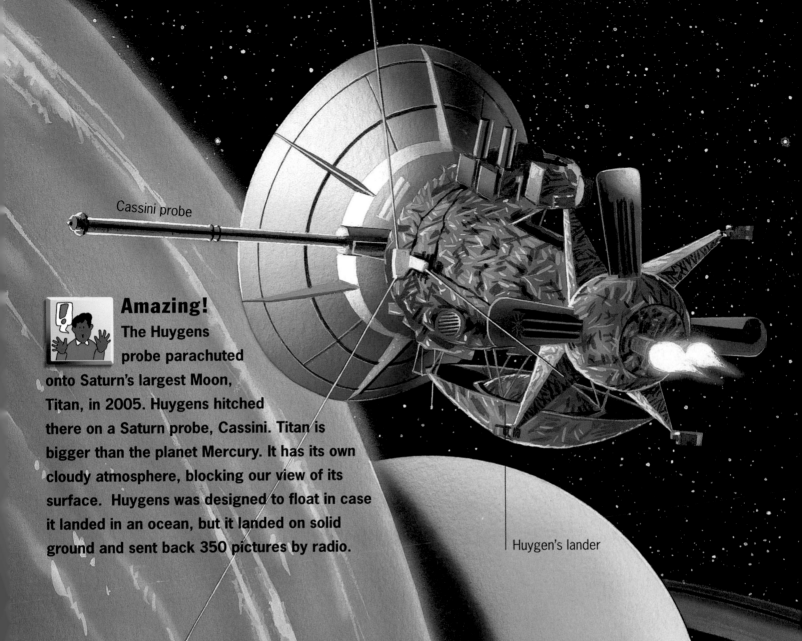

Cassini probe

Amazing!
The Huygens probe parachuted onto Saturn's largest Moon, Titan, in 2005. Huygens hitched there on a Saturn probe, Cassini. Titan is bigger than the planet Mercury. It has its own cloudy atmosphere, blocking our view of its surface. Huygens was designed to float in case it landed in an ocean, but it landed on solid ground and sent back 350 pictures by radio.

Huygen's lander

? Which probe visited a comet?

Giotto was made to visit Halley's Comet as it passed Earth in 1986. Giotto had a special shield to protect it from the dust of the comet's tail. The probe took measurements and photographs from 370 miles away, revealing the rocky heart of the comet.

Giotto passing Halley's Comet

Is it true?
There is life on Mars.

NO. Probes have tested Martian soil for life. They added food to the soil to see if there was anything living there that was hungry! There wasn't. Then scientists found what looked like fossils inside a rock from Mars. After careful checking, they decided that the shapes were probably odd-looking crystals. So there is no life on Mars, unless it is very good at hiding from us!

What bounced around on Mars?

The Mars Pathfinder probe dropped onto Mars inside a bundle of balloons. The balloons bounced away from the falling parachute, deflated, then the Sojourner rover slowly drove away over them.

Who drove a vehicle on Mars?

The Mars Pathfinder (1997) had a small, six-wheeled rover called Sojourner. It used a camera and laser beams to find its way. In 2004, two larger rovers, Spirit and Opportunity, landed on Mars. They have made many exciting discoveries—but no signs of life.

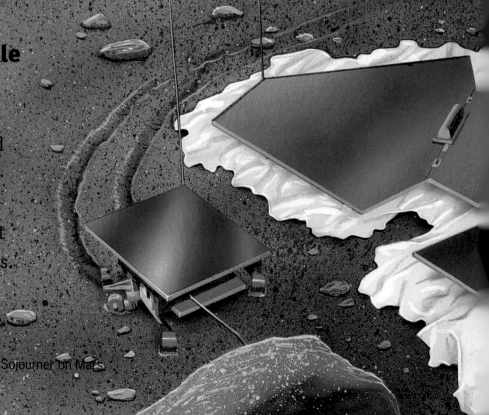

Sojourner on Mars

? Did Vikings really land on Mars?

Two space probes, called Viking 1 and Viking 2, landed on Mars in the 1970s. They took 3,000 photos, some in three dimensions, and beamed them back to Earth. The probes also measured weather patterns and examined the soil for signs of life. They didn't find any aliens.

Mars Pathfinder landing

Mars probe

 Amazing! For 20 years before Pathfinder, several probes sent to Mars ended in disaster. A total of 16 probes from Russia either exploded on launch, missed the planet, or crashed into its surface. The American probe Observer exploded as it entered Mars's orbit. Some probes just went missing. Nobody knows why.

245

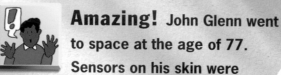 **Amazing!** John Glenn went to space at the age of 77. Sensors on his skin were used to monitor his health. His record-breaking flight happened 36 years after his first space trip, when he was the first American to orbit the Earth.

John Glenn

? Who is building a new space station?

A group of countries is building an International Space Station (ISS). Parts are made in the United States, Japan, Russia, Canada, and Europe and are taken up by various crafts. ISS uses giant solar panels to make its own electricity.

International Space Station

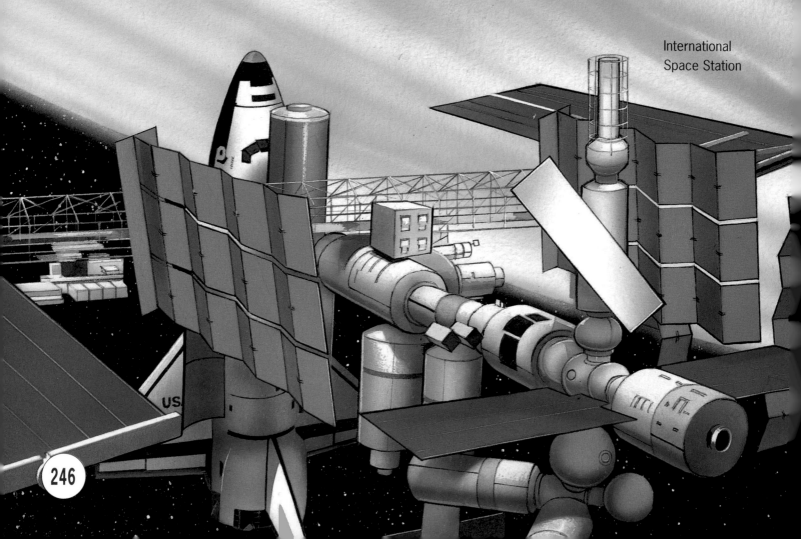

? Will there ever be a Moon base?

If space gets a lot busier, it will make sense to use the Moon as a base. The Moon's low gravity lets big spacecraft take off and land easily compared to Earth.

Future Moon base

Is it true?

People can be "buried" in space.

YES. Rockets, such as Pegasus, have made space funerals possible. Pegasus delivered 25 people's ashes into space in 1997. Other burials have also taken place as part of space missions—even on the Moon.

? Will you ever go to space?

Only a few people become astronauts. But some wealthy tourists may now vacation in space. There are plans to use empty shuttle fuel tanks as the rooms of a space hotel!

Space hotel of the future

Millennium Bird
X-33
United States

VentureStar

? What will spacecraft be like in the future?

Space shuttles will be replaced very soon with new craft. The United States is developing the Orion spacecraft, which is in some ways similar to the Apollo Moonships. It will be launched by a new rocket, Ares 1, while the bigger Ares 5 rocket will take up unmanned cargoes.

 Will we ever visit other solar systems?

The nearest star to our Sun is 4.3 light-years away. The shuttle would take 158,000 years to get there! We will need amazing new spacecraft before we visit other solar systems.

 Amazing! You might travel to space on a laser beam! Scientists in the United States are testing a laser that heats a pocket of air under a spacecraft. The hot air pushes the craft upward. No energy is wasted lifting heavy fuel off the ground.

Spacecraft of the distant future

Colonizing Mars

Will we colonize Mars?

Robots might be able to build a Mars base. Humans would have to wear space suits outside, but would live in airtight habitats, with plants and animals. Genetically modified plants could grow, which would create breathable air and water, making the whole planet habitable.

Pneumatic Worked by air pressure, or containing air.

Pollution The mess caused by fuel-burning machines and human activities, which can be dangerous.

Propeller A set of blades. When a ship's propeller spins around in the water, it pushes the ship along.

Radar A machine that sends radio waves and works out where objects are by detecting how the waves bounce back.

Radiation Dangerous rays, for example those from the Sun. On Earth, the atmosphere blocks most of the Sun's radiation, but in space special shields are needed.

Radiator Part of the cooling system of a car. Air flowing past the radiator cools hot water that has taken heat from the engine.

Rechargeable Describes a battery that can have its electricity replaced after it has run down. All cars have a rechargeable battery.

Roll cage A strong metal frame that surrounds the driver of a car. If a car flips upside down, the roll cage makes the car roll over into an upright position.

Rudder A flap at the stern of a ship or boat that turns from side to side to make the ship or boat turn left or right.

Seaplane An airplane with a boat-shape fuselage, for landing on water.

Sidecar A single-wheeled car with a seat that attaches to the side of a motorcycle.

Space station A huge satellite with living space for a crew of astronauts and scientists.

Stabilizers Small extra wheels on each side of a motorcycle that stop it from toppling over sideways.

Steam engine A type of engine in which the pistons are moved inside cylinders by the pressure of steam created in a boiler.

Stern The back part of a ship.

Supercharger A mechanical pump that increases the amount of air taken into an engine to make it more powerful.

Suspension The springs and shock absorbers on the underside of a vehicle. The suspension allows the vehicle to travel comfortably over bumps on the road.

Tar A black, sticky, waterproof substance that becomes runny when it is heated up and hardens again when it cools.

Throttle The device on a car or motorcycle, also known as the accelerator, which controls the flow of fuel to the engine.

Torpedo An underwater missile that explodes when it hits something.

Tractor unit The front section of an articulated truck, where the cab and engine are located.

Trailer The rear section of an articulated truck, where the cargo is carried.

Trams Electric trains that run in city streets, cleaner and quieter than buses.

Tread The pattern of grooves around the outside of a tire.

Tricycle A bicycle or motorcycle with three wheels, normally one at the front and two at the rear.

Triplane An airplane with three sets of wings.

Undercarriage
The lower section of an airplane. The undercarriage of most planes is the wheels, but seaplanes have floats, and ski planes land using skis.

Index

Ader, Clément 192
Aerocar 82
aircraft carrier 62, 204
air-cushion trains 128
airport tug 189
airships 196
Alcock and Brown 199
Aldrin, Buzz 228
Alien 31
All Terrain Vehicles 27
Alvin 69
ambulance 185
Amphicar 91
anchor 52
Apollo missions 91, 224, 228, 229
armored motorcycles 149
armored personnel carrier 172
armored trains 121
Armstrong, Neil 228
articulated truck 164
Aso Boy 125
Aston Martin DB5 96
Auburn Speedster 79
Austin Landaulet 75
Austin Seven 76
Austin-Healey 3000 95
Austin-Healey Sprite 88

backhoe loader 176
barge 56
barnstormers 199
bathyscaphe 69
battleship 63
Beatles 97
Belgian Bullet 30
Belgian FN 136
Bentley 4.5 liter 78
Bentley Boys 78
Benz Patent-Motorwagen 73
Benz, Karl 72–3
Blériot, Louis 195
Blue Flame 14
BMW C1 157
boilers 106
Bond, James 96
Box Hill Tunnel 119
brakes 113
Braun, Wernher von 223
Brough Superior 138
Brunel, I.K. 51, 118, 119
bubble car 84
Bugatti Royale 77
bullet trains 126, 128, 129
Buran 232
buses 163
Byrd, Richard E. 200

cable cars 116
cab-over truck 165
Cadillac Coupe de Ville 82
Cadillac V-16 79
car transporter 186
cargo aircraft 210
Cassini probe 243
catamaran 36, 57
Catch Me Who Can 103
caterpillar tracks 173
cement mixer 177
"centipede" 108
chaldrons 112

Challenger 14
Channel Tunnel 118, 123
charabanc 77, 163
chariot racing 12
cherry picker 189
Chitty Chitty Bang Bang 97
chopper 152–53
citizens' band radio 166
Citroën 7CV 80
Clancy, Carl Stevens 142
clipper 46
Club Med 52
Collins, Michael 228
Collins, Russ 153
container ship 55
convertibles 79, 89
Copeland, Lucius 134
coracle 43
corsairs 48
crash tests 92
Crossley limousine 91
Cugnot, Nicolas-Joseph 162
curragh 43
custom cars 86
custom truck 169

d'Abbans, Jouffroy 50
Daimler, Gottlieb 72, 135
Davidson, William, Walter
  and Arthur 138
de Dion 13

de Havilland Comet 38
Deep Flight 1 68
demolition derby 32
diesel engine 164, 166
diesel trains 108–9
Diesel, Rudolph 164
digger 174, 176
dinghy 64
dining cars 112
Douglas 137
dragster truck 170
dragsters 22, 23, 153, 170
dugout canoe 42–43
dumper truck 175

E Class 108
ejector seat 233
electric racers 30–31
electric trains 110–11
elevated railroad 119
excavator 174

factory ship 58
Ferrari 360 Modena 89
fifth wheel 164
fighters 208–9
figurehead 46
fire truck 170, 182
fireboxes 106
first flights
 airplane 192
 airship 196
 America to Australia 201
 autogyro 217
 controlled 194
 cross-channel 195
 England to Australia 201
 helicopter 216
 manned 192

nonstop around–the–world in
 balloon 197
 solo around–the–world 201
 solo transatlantic 200
 transatlantic 199
flying boat 202, 210
Flying Fortress 204
flags 20
FN 136
Foden steam truck 162
Ford Mustang 89
Ford Thunderbird 83
Ford V-8 79
Ford, Henry 75
forklift truck 184
Formula One 16, 17

four-wheel drive 179
Free, Rollie 139

Gagarin, Yuri 226
galleon 47
galley 45, 48
garbage truck 189
gears 95, 166
Giffard, Henri 196
Giotto probe 243
Glenn, John 226, 246
gliders 193, 218, 219
Gobron-Brillié 15
go-kart racing 16
Goddard, Robert 222
gondola 44
Grand Prix 28
Grave Digger 169
Gravity Formula One 33
Great Eastern 51
Great Train Robbery 122
Great Wall of China 226
Gresley, Herbert 107
Ground Control 229
gunpowder 222

half-track 173
hang glider 218
Harley, William 138
Harley-Davidson 138, 142, 148
 Electra Glide 142
 WLA 45 148
Harrier attack aircraft 214
helicopters 216–17
Hero of Alexander 103
Heyerdahl, Thor 42
Heysercycle 157
Hollywood 79
Honda Gold Wing 143
 Super Cub 144
 CB750 151
 Elf Endurance 156
horse-drawn wagon 162
horseless carriage 72
hot-air balloons 192, 197, 219
hovercraft 35, 57
Hubble telescope 240–41
Huygens probe 243
hydrofoil 56

ice breaker 54
iceboats 37
Indian Scout 139
in-flight refueling 208
Issigonis, Alec 85

jackknife 167
Jaguar E-type 88
James's steam carriage 72
Jason Junior 69
Jeep 90
jet aircraft 206, 207, 208
jet engines 207, 225